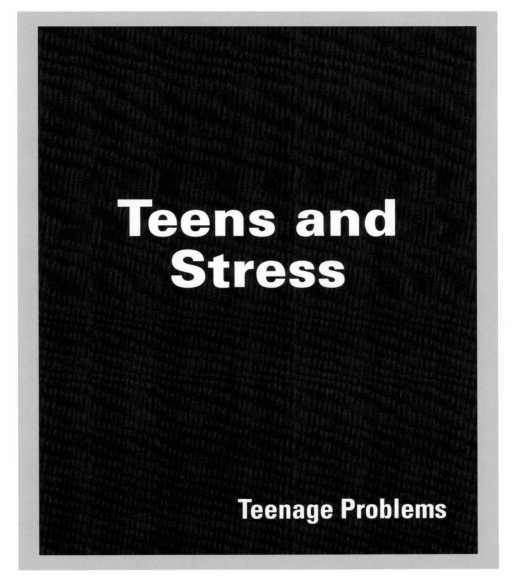

Teens and Stress

Teenage Problems

ReferencePoint
Press®

San Diego, CA

Other books in the Compact Research Teenage Problems set:

Teen Violence
Teenage Alcoholism
Teenage Dropouts
Teenage Drug Abuse
Teenage Eating Disorders
Teenage Sex and Pregnancy
Teenage Suicide
Teens and Cheating
Teens: Cutting and Self-Injury

*For a complete list of titles please visit www.referencepointpress.com.

COMPACT *Research*

Teens and Stress

Peggy J. Parks

Teenage Problems

ReferencePoint
Press®

San Diego, CA

© 2015 ReferencePoint Press, Inc.
Printed in the United States

For more information, contact:
ReferencePoint Press, Inc.
PO Box 27779
San Diego, CA 92198
www.ReferencePointPress.com

Picture credits:
Cover: iStockphoto.com and Thinkstock/Comstock
Maury Aaseng: 31–33, 45–47, 59–61, 73–74
Thinkstock Images: 12, 18

LIBRARY OF CONGRESS CATALOGING-IN-PUBLICATION DATA

Parks, Peggy J., 1951-
  Teens and stress / by Peggy J. Parks.
    pages cm. -- (Compact research)
  Includes bibliographical references and index.
  ISBN 978-1-60152-768-4 (hardback) -- ISBN 1-60152-768-3 (hardback)
    1. Stress in adolescence--Juvenile literature. 2. Stress management for teenagers--Juvenile
literature. 3. Stress (Psychology)--Juvenile literature. 4. Teenagers--Health and hygiene--
Juvenile literature. I. Title.
  BF724.3.S86P37   2015
  155.5'189042--dc23
                                                   2014036018

Contents

Foreword

As modern civilization continues to evolve, its ability to create, store, distribute, and access information expands exponentially. The explosion of information from all media continues to increase at a phenomenal rate. By 2020 some experts predict the worldwide information base will double every seventy-three days. While access to diverse sources of information and perspectives is paramount to any democratic society, information alone cannot help people gain knowledge and understanding. Information must be organized and presented clearly and succinctly in order to be understood. The challenge in the digital age becomes not the creation of information, but how best to sort, organize, enhance, and present information.

ReferencePoint Press developed the *Compact Research* series with this challenge of the information age in mind. More than any other subject area today, researching current issues can yield vast, diverse, and unqualified information that can be intimidating and overwhelming for even the most advanced and motivated researcher. The *Compact Research* series offers a compact, relevant, intelligent, and conveniently organized collection of information covering a variety of current topics ranging from illegal immigration and deforestation to diseases such as anorexia and meningitis.

The series focuses on three types of information: objective single-author narratives, opinion-based primary source quotations, and facts and statistics. The clearly written objective narratives provide context and reliable background information. Primary source quotes are carefully selected and cited, exposing the reader to differing points of view, and facts and statistics sections aid the reader in evaluating perspectives. Presenting these key types of information creates a richer, more balanced learning experience.

For better understanding and convenience, the series enhances information by organizing it into narrower topics and adding design features that make it easy for a reader to identify desired content. For example, in *Compact Research: Illegal Immigration*, a chapter covering the economic impact of illegal immigration has an objective narrative explaining the various ways the economy is impacted, a balanced section of numerous primary source quotes on the topic, followed by facts and full-color illustrations to encourage evaluation of contrasting perspectives.

The ancient Roman philosopher Lucius Annaeus Seneca wrote, "It is quality rather than quantity that matters." More than just a collection of content, the *Compact Research* series is simply committed to creating, finding, organizing, and presenting the most relevant and appropriate amount of information on a current topic in a user-friendly style that invites, intrigues, and fosters understanding.

Stress at a Glance

Stress Defined

Stress is a thought or feeling that occurs in response to a perceived challenge or threat known as a stressor.

Fight or Flight

The body's instinctive mechanism for staying to face a challenge or threat or running away from it is known as the fight-or-flight response.

Beneficial Stress

Stress is often perceived only as harmful, but it can also energize people and motivate them to take action.

Stress Overload

When stress weighs teens down, their symptoms may include trouble concentrating, difficulty sleeping at night, and increased irritability and moodiness.

Teens at Risk

Gay and lesbian teens have a higher likelihood of stress overload than straight teens because of rejection and discrimination.

Health Issues

Stress-related health problems include headaches, stomachaches and other digestive problems, impaired immunity to illness, and depression.

Unhealthy Efforts to Cope

In trying to feel better, teens may turn to drinking, drugs, or smoking, as well as deliberately injuring themselves through cutting or other methods.

Healthy Coping Mechanisms

Tactics for managing stress include getting enough sleep, keeping a manageable schedule, and exercising regularly.

Overview

"Just being a teen can be stressful—there is so much going on and so many changes that are happening all at once!"

—Office on Women's Health, which works to improve the health and well-being of women and girls in the United States.

"We generally use the word 'stress' when we feel that everything seems to have become too much—we are overloaded and wonder whether we really can cope with the pressures placed upon us."

—Christian Nordqvist, editor and cofounder of Medical News Today.

Blake Kernen is a New Jersey teenager who knows how stressful it is to be pulled in too many different directions. She also knows that stress overload can make her sick—because it has. Kernen's schedule is jam-packed, with little free time left over. "I consider myself to be pretty busy," she says, "engaged in some sort of activity most of the time. Being a 14-year-old, that's the way it is for me and for most of my friends these days."[1] Along with school and homework, Kernen plays guitar, is involved in tennis and other extracurricular activities, maintains and writes her own blog, and participates in community service projects. She is so busy that she feels lucky to find time to hang out with her friends and family. But, she says, "I'm not complaining because I love doing everything that I have to do, except maybe the homework."[2]

There are times, however, when Kernen says it feels good not to have anything on her schedule—a day that is all hers, with nothing planned.

For that reason she is delighted when school is canceled because of snowy or icy weather. "It's not that I'm in love with winter," she says, "but I do appreciate what comes along with it: Snow days, guilt-free, lazy no-school days. Days when you can kick back, relax and do anything you want and in my case, that's pretty close to nothing at all."[3]

Stretched Too Thin

Now more than ever Kernen realizes the value of having downtime: days when she can do exactly what she feels like doing, rather than having all her time allocated. She never gave much thought to stress until she had crammed so much into her schedule that she started getting sick. "I realized I had way too much going on—concert, paper, test, competition—the pressure and stress of it made me feel sick to my stomach," she says. "I couldn't eat or sleep. And trying to do it all on not enough sleep made matters even worse. I was clearly on edge and anxious."[4]

Knowing that something had to give, Kernen talked with her parents about how she was feeling. With their full support she dropped some activities and kept only those that were most important to her. "Instantly, I felt a sense of relief," she says. Kernen urges other young people not to overload themselves so much that they miss out on the fun things in life. "Being an over-scheduled teen today is not uncommon, but it is something that we, as teens, need to be aware of, for the sake of our health and for our sanity," she says. "Take time for yourself to do the things you love or sometimes to just not do anything at all."[5]

What Is Stress?

The pressure that was weighing Kernen down is not uncommon among young people today. They become stressed-out from tough school demands, overpacked schedules, relationship issues, the pressure of trying to fit in with peers, and/or an unhappy home environment. On top of all that, teens must cope with the hormonal changes that come with puberty. "The early teen years are marked by rapid changes—physical, cognitive, and emotional," says the Johns Hopkins Bloomberg School of Public Health. "Young people also face changing relationships with peers, new demands at school, family tensions, and safety issues in their communities. The ways in which teens cope with these stressors can have significant short- and long-term consequences on their physical and emotional health."[6]

Many teens feel pressure to do well on tests and papers at school, but sometimes the stress becomes overwhelming when they try to cram too many activities into their schedules. Too little sleep, a common problem for busy teens, only makes matters worse.

As serious and troubling as stress can be for teens, they may be surprised to learn that it is actually just a thought or feeling. The discomfort that is associated with stress is caused by someone's reaction to whatever caused the thought or feeling, which is known as a stressor. Being aware of this helps explain why things that are considered stressful often differ from one person to another. A teen who perceives something as a threat or challenge, for instance, may become stressed over it, whereas his or her classmate may not find it stressful at all. To illustrate this concept in a way that is relevant to young people, Johns Hopkins Bloomberg School of Public Health shares a scenario about teens at a high school dance:

> Some are hunched in the corner, eyes downcast and hugging the wall. They can't wait for the night to be over. Others are out there dancing their feet off, talking and laughing and hoping the music never stops. In between,

you may find a few kids pretending to be bored, hanging out with their friends, and maybe venturing onto the floor for a dance or two. So, is the dance uniformly stressful?[7]

When someone is overloaded with stress, both external and internal factors are involved. *External* refers to factors in the person's physical environment such as school, sports, hobbies and other activities, job, relationships with others, and home life. In addition, says physician and medical journalist Melissa Conrad Stöppler, external factors include "all the situations, challenges, difficulties, and expectations you're confronted with on a daily basis." In contrast, internal factors—including overall health and fitness, nutritional status, emotional well-being, and the amount of rest and sleep the person gets—affect his or her reaction to stress-inducing external factors. "The management of stress," says Stöppler, "is mostly dependent on the ability and willingness of a person to make the changes necessary for a healthy lifestyle."[8]

> " The discomfort that is associated with stress is caused by someone's reaction to whatever caused the thought or feeling, which is known as a stressor. "

Stay or Run Away?

Whenever humans are faced with a situation they perceive as a challenge or threat, they have a built-in mechanism for handling it called the fight-or-flight response. This is so named because it causes people to instinctively decide whether to stay and deal with the threat or to take flight (run away) from it. Medical News Today cofounder and editor Christian Nordqvist explains: "If you are upstairs at home and an earthquake starts, the faster you can get yourself and your family out the more likely you are all to survive. If you need to save somebody's life during that earthquake, by lifting a heavy weight that has fallen on them, you will need components in your body to be activated to give you that extra strength—that extra push."[9]

The physical process of fight or flight begins when the perceived threat or challenge triggers the sympathetic nervous system to kick into gear. Stress hormones are released into the bloodstream, causing heart rate, blood pressure, and metabolism to speed up. Muscles tense, senses sharpen, and the person becomes hyperalert and focused. Nordqvist explains: "Non-essential body functions slow down, such as our digestive and immune systems when we are in fight-or-flight response mode. All resources can then be concentrated on rapid breathing, blood flow, alertness and muscle use."[10] This combination of physical factors, says Nordqvist, is what helps people protect themselves in dangerous or challenging situations.

Good Stress

When teens talk to each other about stress in their lives, they usually are not referring to something that makes them happy. But stress is not always harmful; in fact, people rely on it for survival. "Without stress," says health and science journalist Thea Singer, "we'd be as good as dead. We wouldn't have the gumption to slalom down Whistler's mountains to Olympic gold, to play Juliet to our Romeo, to ask the boss for a raise, or even to get out of bed. That's because stress in appropriate amounts is the very stimulation that keeps us engaged with the world moment to moment."[11]

> "Whenever humans are faced with a situation they perceive as a challenge or threat, they have a built-in mechanism for handling it called the fight-or-flight response.

Although they may not be aware of it, people rely on stress often. When a teenage girl who is vying for an important science award psyches herself up to give a presentation to the judges, that is stress at work. When a teenage boy sits down to take his final exam in advanced placement calculus, stress provides him with the energy and enthusiasm to give it everything he has. The children's health organization Nemours Foundation says that stress is activated in situations like these "when the pressure's on but there's no actual danger—like stepping up to take the foul shot that could win the game, getting ready to go to a big dance, or sitting down for a final exam. A little of this stress can help keep you on your toes, ready to rise to a challenge."[12]

Warning Signs of Stress Overload

Teens can usually tell when they are under too much stress because their bodies let them know. They may feel uncharacteristically irritable, get headaches more often than usual, and have trouble concentrating. Other signs include changes in appetite, feeling sad and weepy, and difficulty sleeping at night. "Everyone experiences stress a little differently," says the Nemours Foundation. "Some people become angry and act out their stress or take it out on others. Some people internalize it and develop eating disorders or substance abuse problems. And some people who have a chronic illness may find that the symptoms of their illness flare up under an overload of stress."[13]

> **Teens can usually tell when they are under too much stress because their bodies let them know.**

Alameda, California, teen Nora Huynh was exhibiting signs of stress overload that worried her mother. The girl was tired a lot of the time, often suffered from headaches, and was growing increasingly irritable toward her siblings. But the biggest red flag was the day Huynh got her report card and was devastated that her grade point average was not a perfect 4.0. Her mother says that Huynh had a "total meltdown, cried for hours. I couldn't believe her reaction."[14]

What Causes Teens to Get Stressed?

Aside from routine causes such as the pressures of school, extracurricular activities, family, and other daily responsibilities, chronic (long-lasting) stress can result from more serious underlying factors. Being bullied is one example; studies have shown that teens who have suffered from bullying often experience high levels of stress. The same is true of teens who struggle with family conflicts; live in dangerous neighborhoods where they do not feel safe; have lived through a traumatic experience such as a house fire, assault, or natural disaster; and/or have been neglected or abused. Also overwhelming and stressful for teens, says the Nemours Foundation, are the "heavy emotions that can accompany a broken heart or the death of a loved one."[15]

A teenage girl who anonymously wrote a chapter for the book *Pressure: True Stories by Teens About Stress* describes how stressful her family life is: "The amount of stress in my home is overwhelming. My stepmother can't deal with her rambunctious kids, and too often she either yells at and hits them, or she just leaves the house and all the responsibilities to me. . . . Sometimes I feel so stressed that I want to scream or run away."[16] The girl wants to be as helpful as she can, but she becomes frustrated and stressed-out when she is expected to handle so much responsibility at her young age. To cope with stress she goes for walks in the park, spends time with her friends, reads, and writes poetry. When the day comes that she is old enough to move away and be on her own, she hopes that "all the frustration, anger, and stress that I've experienced in my house [don't] come with me."[17]

Higher-Risk Teens

Research has shown that certain groups of teens are more vulnerable to stress overload than other young people their age. This is often true of teens with learning disabilities, emotional problems, or anxiety disorders, as the University of Maryland Medical Center explains: "People who are less emotionally stable or who have high anxiety levels tend to experience specific events more stressfully than others."[18]

Gay and lesbian teens have been shown to suffer from a high incidence of physical and mental health problems, which researchers believe is related to what is called minority stress. A May 2014 American Academy of Pediatrics news release explains: "According to this theory, chronic stress due to discrimination, rejection, harassment, concealment of sexual orientation, internalized homophobia (negative attitudes toward homosexuality) and other negative experiences leads to poor health."[19] The validity of the theory was confirmed in a study that was released in May 2014. It involved

> " Gay and lesbian teens have been shown to suffer from a high incidence of physical and mental health problems, which researchers believe is related to what is called minority stress. "

1,232 youth aged twelve to eighteen, of whom 16 percent were lesbian females and 84 percent were gay males. The focus was to determine whether the minority stress theory could explain the higher incidence of binge drinking among gay and lesbian teens compared with heterosexual teens. The study revealed that the reason these teens engaged in heavy drinking was mainly due to chronic stress caused by difficult social experiences such as homophobia and gay or lesbian victimization.

What Health Problems Are Associated with Stress?

Stress is an essential part of being human, and the body is capable of handling it in manageable amounts. "Our goal isn't a life without stress," says Stanford University neurobiologist Robert M. Sepolsky. "The idea is to have the right amount of stress."[20] When stress becomes chronic, however, and is a constant, overbearing presence in someone's life, this can lead to numerous health problems.

Research has shown that stress disrupts the digestive system, which can lead to diarrhea, constipation, cramps, and bloating. It can also cause excessive production of digestive acids in the stomach, leading to a painful burning sensation that is often called heartburn. Also closely related to chronic stress is impaired immune system function, as the American Psychological Association (APA) writes:

> In particular, long-term, high stress can weaken immune systems and exhaust the body. Research also shows that even otherwise healthy teens who experience consistent stress have higher levels of inflammation, which has long been associated with development of cardiovascular disease. Even the common cold is influenced by stress—people living with chronic stress get more frequent and severe viral infections.[21]

Unhealthy Ways of Coping

It is understandable that teens who are deeply troubled by stress want to feel better. It can be extremely difficult to wake up nearly every morning feeling like the pressure and tension are too much to take. To ease the emotional turmoil that is characteristic of severe stress, some teens make unwise choices like smoking or using alcohol or drugs. According

Some teens work out their stress through exercise or by playing video games. Others turn to drugs, alcohol, or cigarettes in hopes of finding relief.

to the Citizens Commission on Human Rights of Florida, some studies have shown that more than 70 percent of teens who use drugs started using them primarily due to worry over school grades. "Discord in the family has also been shown to be a contributing factor to teenage stress," the group writes. "The same study showed that only 7% of parents believe their child became drug dependent due to stress, showing some possible lack of communication between child and parent."[22]

> To ease the emotional turmoil that is characteristic of severe stress, some teens make unwise choices like smoking or using alcohol or drugs.

One finding of a study released in 2014 by the APA was that a high number of teens are relying on sedentary methods of coping with stress, rather than being active and exercising. To manage stress, for instance, 46 percent of teens said they play video games, compared with 37 percent who walk or exercise and 28 percent who play sports. Another finding was that teens who exercise and/or play sports have lower average stress levels than those who are sedentary. The 2014 report offers an example: "Almost half of teens with high stress (48 percent) say they watch television or movies for more than two hours a day. Only 20 percent of teens with low stress do the same."[23]

Stress and Self-Injury

Research has shown a strong link between stress overload in teens and the practice of deliberately injuring themselves. Known as self-injury, self-harm, self-mutilation, or simply "cutting," the practice is most prevalent among teens who are stressed and also suffer from a great deal of emotional pain. One of clinical psychologist Lucie Hemmen's patients, Molly, is a classic example of a teenage girl with a high-stress life. She works hard at her studies, gets excellent grades, and is involved in a number of extracurricular activities—too many, in fact. She crammed so much into her schedule that before long, she found nothing enjoyable anymore.

Eventually, Molly found the stress too much to bear, and she started cutting herself. She explains:

> It started as an impulse. Of course I know a lot of girls who cut so the idea came to me and I started with a paper clip. I ran it along the inside of my arm until it made a mark. Then I went deeper until I made myself bleed. It was totally engrossing and I can't explain why but it made me feel better. I graduated to straight edge razors and, at the time, it seemed perfectly fine to me. It was a little secret compartment of my life where I had all the power and control.[24]

How Can Teens Cope with Stress?

There are numerous steps teens can take to manage their stress and keep it under control. One simple but essential step is making sure they get enough sleep at night, but this often does not happen. The National Sleep Foundation writes: "Teens need about 9¼ hours of sleep each night to function best (for some, 8½ hours is enough). Most teens do not

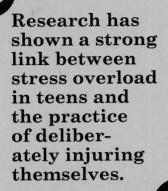

> **Research has shown a strong link between stress overload in teens and the practice of deliberately injuring themselves.**

get enough sleep—one study found that only 15% reported sleeping 8½ hours on school nights."[25] The 2014 APA study clearly showed the benefits of sleep for teens. The researchers found that teens with low levels of stress sleep 7.8 hours per night, compared with 6.9 hours per night for teens with high stress levels.

Tactics that can help young people manage stress include refraining from overscheduling, learning and practicing relaxation techniques, getting rid of negative thinking, and taking steps to be healthier and fitter. Being proactive is the key to managing stress, as the Nemours Foundation explains: "Knowing how to 'de-stress' and doing it when things are relatively calm can help you get through challenging circumstances that may arise."[26]

Just Part of Being Human

It is a proven fact that today's teens are stressed, although their reasons may not be the same. Some overload themselves with extracurricular activities and have a difficult time balancing that with school and homework. Others are stressed because of bullying, their family situation, relationship issues, or other conflicts. The right amount of stress is beneficial, because it allows humans young and old to survive and thrive—but too much can be detrimental to anyone's well-being. By adopting healthy ways of coping with stress and practicing them regularly, teens can learn to keep their stress levels under control.

What Is Stress?

"Stress can be compared with the pressure that a sculptor places on a piece of marble: the right pressure and it becomes a masterpiece, but too much pressure and the marble breaks into pieces."

—Luz Ayda Krafsig, a physician and science writer for the National Science Foundation.

"Most teens experience more stress when they perceive a situation as dangerous, difficult, or painful and they do not have the resources to cope."

—American Academy of Child & Adolescent Psychiatry, which seeks to promote the health and well-being of children, adolescents, and families.

During the 1920s, when scientist Hans Selye was still a medical student in Prague, Czechoslovakia, he became aware of a puzzling medical condition. Selye observed that patients with a variety of diseases exhibited identical signs and symptoms of an entirely separate ailment. "Whether a man suffers from a loss of blood, an infectious disease, or advanced cancer," Selye wrote, "he loses his appetite, his muscle strength, and his ambition to accomplish anything; usually the patient also loses weight and even his facial expression betrays that he is ill." For lack of a better term, Selye referred to the mysterious ailment as "the syndrome of just being sick." Later he began calling it "stress."[27]

Groundbreaking Studies

Selye was interested in pursuing research on the peculiar syndrome, but he was still in medical school and could not muster support from his adviser. So he put his research goals aside for nearly a decade. Then during the 1930s, when Selye was working at McGill University in Montreal, Canada, he was finally able to focus on stress research. It was at McGill that he conducted his now famous stress experiments with laboratory rats.

On July 4, 1936, the British scientific journal *Nature* published a short paper Selye had written titled "A Syndrome Produced by Diverse Nocuous Agents." In the paper Selye gave a detailed account of his experiments, describing how he had subjected rats to stimuli such as extreme temperatures of hot and cold, deafening noise, severe hunger, excessive exercise, and blinding light. He then euthanized the rats so he could examine their internal organs. What Selye found was surprising: No matter what sort of pain or frustration he had inflicted on the creatures, the physical effects were the same, as medical historian Mark Jackson explains: "Almost universally these rats showed a particular set of signs. There would be changes particularly in the adrenal gland. So Selye began to suggest that subjecting an animal to prolonged stress led to tissue changes and physiological changes with the release of certain hormones, that would then cause disease and ultimately the death of the animal."[28]

> **For lack of a better term, Selye referred to the mysterious ailment as 'the syndrome of just being sick.' Later he began calling it 'stress.'**

From his laboratory experiments with animals, Selye was able to confirm his long-held theory that stress played a major role in the development of disease. Because of his past observations of patients with various illnesses also getting sick with a companion ailment, he had no doubt that stress caused illness in humans as well. Yet even though he was the first scientist to show the harmful effects of stress, he considered it equally important for people to understand that stress was not always damaging. On the contrary, it could be beneficial, acting as an energizing and motivating force. Since he knew that stress was typically viewed in a negative light, Selye referred to it by using different words. He coined the terms *stressor* to define whatever stimulus provoked a stressful response and *eustress* to signify beneficial, energy-producing stress. In reference to unpleasant, illness-producing stress, Selye used the existing term *distress*. "He wrote that the body undergoes virtually the same nonspecific response during eustress and distress," says Wayne State University researcher Virginia Hill Rice. "In the former, however, there is much less damage."[29]

Even though much of Selye's professional career was devoted to conducting and writing about stress-related research, he was the first to admit that stress was a difficult concept to define. According to his friend and professional colleague Paul J. Rosche, who is also a noted stress researcher, Selye "struggled unsuccessfully all his life to find a satisfactory definition of stress. In attempting to extrapolate his animal studies to humans so that people would understand what he meant, he redefined stress as 'The rate of wear and tear on the body.'" Rosche adds that in Selye's later years, "when asked to define stress, he told reporters, 'Everyone knows what stress is, but nobody really knows.'"[30]

Fight or Flight

The concept of stress being good as well as bad is important because stress not only invigorates and energizes people, it can save their lives. This aspect of stress, known as the fight-or-flight response, is described by the American Academy of Child & Adolescent Psychiatry: "When we perceive a situation as difficult or painful, changes occur in our minds and bodies to prepare us to respond to danger. This 'fight, flight, or freeze' response includes faster heart and breathing rate, increased blood to muscles of arms and legs, cold or clammy hands and feet, upset stomach and/or a sense of dread."[31]

The fight-or-flight response was identified by Harvard University physiologist Walter Bradford Cannon years before Selye conducted his research. While studying laboratory animals, Cannon observed that the creatures underwent distinct physical changes when they were frightened, excited, or angry. These changes were

> " The concept of stress being good as well as bad is important because stress not only invigorates and energizes people, it can save their lives. "

not a conscious effort on the part of the animals; rather, they were solely based on instinct, as Cannon explained in his 1915 book *Bodily Changes in Pain, Hunger, Fear and Rage*: "The most significant feature of these bodily reactions in pain and in the presence of emotion-provoking objects is that they are of the nature of reflexes—they are not willed movements, indeed they are often distressingly beyond the control of the will."[32]

> " Ancient humans were prey for all kinds of fierce creatures roaming the earth, from snarling saber-toothed tigers to huge predatory birds and ferocious cave bears. "

Cannon observed that the physiological changes in the animals' bodies were the result of a surge of chemical activity in the bloodstream. This provided an animal with the physical resources necessary to resolve a particular threat, either by fighting it or running away from it. "The reflex response," Cannon wrote, "is precisely what would be most serviceable to the organism in the strenuous efforts of fighting or escape that might accompany or follow distress or fear or rage."[33] Cannon went on to explain that the fight-or-flight mechanism worked in a nearly identical way for human beings as for other types of animals.

Inside the Stressed Body

Modern humans may not rely heavily on the fight-or-flight response, but to those living in ancient times it meant the difference between life and death. Ancient humans were prey for all kinds of fierce creatures roaming the earth, from snarling saber-toothed tigers and huge predatory birds to ferocious cave bears. In an October 2012 *Salon* article, University of North Carolina biologist and science author Rob Dunn writes:

> When we saw or heard a sign of danger—a movement in the grass, a strange shadow—hormonal reactions screamed out inside our bodies. These fight-or-flight responses sped up the heart, increased blood flow to muscles, caused hyperventilation (to get more oxygen for quick reaction),

and made us more likely to respond quickly to a predator
by searching for it, hiding, running away, or for the truly
brave, throwing a stick and then running away.[34]

Even though humans today do not face the fierce, numerous preda-
tors of ancient times, the human body still has essentially the same reaction to stressful situations. Whenever any sort of threat is perceived, such
as a car speeding toward pedestrians at a crosswalk, the eyes and ears
instantly transmit the information to the brain's amygdala, an almond-
shaped mass of nerve cells that contributes to emotional processing. In
turn the amygdala interprets the images and sounds, as an article in the
March 2011 *Harvard Mental Health Letter* explains: "When it perceives
danger, it instantly sends a distress signal to the hypothalamus." This is
the part of the brain that is responsible for hormone production and
maintaining the body's homeostasis, meaning its internal balance. The
Harvard article continues: "This area of the brain functions like a command center, communicating with the rest of the body through the nervous system so that the person has the energy to fight or flee."[35]

Specifically, this "command center" communicates through the autonomic nervous system, which regulates the functions of internal organs
such as the heart, stomach, and intestines. The autonomic nervous system has two components: the sympathetic nervous system and the parasympathetic nervous system. "The sympathetic nervous system functions
like a gas pedal in a car," says the Harvard article. "It triggers the fight-
or-flight response, providing the body with a burst of energy so that it
can respond to perceived dangers."[36] A surge of chemical changes begins
taking place instantaneously as bursts of stress hormones such as adrenaline and cortisol are released into the bloodstream. "All of these changes
happen so quickly that people aren't aware of them," says the Harvard
article. "In fact, the wiring is so efficient that the amygdala and hypothalamus start this cascade even before the brain's visual centers have had
a chance to fully process what is happening. That's why people are able
to jump out of the path of an oncoming car even before they think about
what they are doing."[37]

The article goes on to say that the parasympathetic nervous system
functions much like the brake pedal of a car. Once the perceived danger has
passed, its function is to slow the heart rate, decrease blood pressure, and

in general help return the body to its normal state of relaxation and calm. Continuing with the car analogy, in people who are chronically stressed, either the "gas pedal" is stuck or the "brakes" are not working properly.

Stressed-Out Teens

Studies have shown that adults in America have high stress levels, which is due to a number of factors. According to the February 2014 APA *Stress in America* study, issues related to money, work, and the economy were the most commonly mentioned stressors for adults. But the same study revealed that teens are just as stressed-out as adults—and in some cases even more so. In an article about the study, Boston pediatrician Claire McCarthy writes, "Adults are the ones who are supposed to be stressed, not kids. Childhood is supposed to be the stress-free part of life, right? Well, maybe not. At least not for teens."[38]

The *Stress in America* study found that teens' experiences with stress are similar to those of adults. In fact, during the school year the average stress level of teens is actually higher than levels reported by adults. Participants were asked to use a scale of 1 to 10, with 1 meaning no stress at all and 10 indicating extremely high stress levels. With a healthy stress level being approximately 3.9, teens averaged 5.8 and adults averaged 5.1. During the summer months, the study found that 13 percent of teens experienced stress at extreme levels of 8, 9, or 10 on a 10-point scale. "Teens report being more stressed than they think is healthy," says McCarthy. "More during the school year, but also during the summer when theoretically, they should be relaxing."[39]

During the study, when asked specific questions about their experiences during the previous month, nearly one-third of the teens reported feeling overwhelmed, depressed, or sad as a result of stress. Few teens said that their stress was declining: Only 16 percent reported that their

> **When asked specific questions about their experiences during the previous month, nearly one-third of the teens reported feeling overwhelmed, depressed, or sad as a result of stress.**

stress levels were lower than they were the year before, compared with 31 percent who said their stress had increased in the past year. More than one-third of the teens believed that their stress levels would increase in the following year. "We need to take stress in teenagers very seriously," says Norman Anderson, president of the APA. "Those adolescents who report high levels of stress are also reporting high levels of anxiety, high levels of anger, high levels of irritability."[40]

A Complex Phenomenon

Stress is a topic that is challenging for many people to understand—even the renowned scientist Hans Selye himself acknowledged how difficult it was to define. Thanks to his research, though, as well as studies conducted by Cannon and other noted scientists, it is now known that the effects of stress can range from harmful to beneficial and life saving. In addition, scientists understand the physiological process of the stress response. There is a great deal more to be learned, however, such as why teens are starting to show levels of stress equal to or exceeding the levels of adults. In the future, these and other puzzling mysteries related to stress may eventually be resolved through research.

Primary Source Quotes*

What Is Stress?

❝You may think that modern advances in science and technology should have resulted in lower stress levels. Clearly this hasn't happened—for anybody.❞

—Allen Elkin, *Stress Management for Dummies*. Hoboken, NJ: Wiley, 2013, p. 1.

Elkin is a clinical psychologist who practices in New York City.

❝Evidence is mounting that this generation of young people experiences more stress than any previous generation.❞

—Kara E. Powell, "4 Steps to Help a Stressed Teenager," *FYI* (blog), February 27, 2014. http://fulleryouthinstitute.org.

Powell is an educator, professor, author, and executive director of the youth ministry organization Fuller Youth Institute.

❝Adolescent boys and girls experience equal amounts of stress, but the source and effects may differ.❞

—University of Maryland Medical Center, "Stress," June 26, 2013. http://umm.edu.

Located in downtown Baltimore, the University of Maryland Medical Center is one of the oldest academic medical centers in the United States.

* Editor's Note: While the definition of a primary source can be narrowly or broadly defined, for the purposes of Compact Research, a primary source consists of: 1) results of original research presented by an organization or researcher; 2) eyewitness accounts of events, personal experience, or work experience; 3) first-person editorials offering pundits' opinions; 4) government officials presenting political plans and/or policies; 5) representatives of organizations presenting testimony or policy.

66 **What some find stressful, others find exciting, and yet others may be unaffected.** **99**

—Rick Harrington, *Stress, Health and Well-Being: Thriving in the 21st Century*. Belmont, CA: Wadsworth, 2013, p. 23.

Harrington is a psychologist, researcher, and university professor from Houston, Texas.

66 **Stress results from believing the negative stories that our egoic mind, the voice in our head, tells us about ourselves, life, others, the past, the present or the future.** **99**

—Gina Lake, *From Stress to Stillness: Tools for Inner Peace*. Sedona, AZ: Endless Satsang Foundation, 2013, p. 2.

Lake holds a master's degree in counseling psychology and has written a number of books about stress, wellness, and happiness.

66 **Stress is a normal feeling. In small amounts, stress can help you get things done.** **99**

—Fred K. Berger, "Stress and Anxiety," MedlinePlus, February 24, 2014. www.nlm.nih.gov.

Berger is an addiction and forensic psychiatrist at Scripps Memorial Hospital in La Jolla, California.

66 **Anything that poses a challenge or a threat to our well-being is a stress.** **99**

—Christian Nordqvist, "What Is Stress? How to Deal with Stress," *Medical News Today*, July 30, 2014. www.medicalnewstoday.com.

Nordqvist is cofounder and editor of Medical News Today.

66 **It can be very tough when more than one stressful event happens at the same time or stress is ongoing.** **99**

—Office on Women's Health, "Feeling Stressed," April 9, 2014. http://girlshealth.gov.

The Office on Women's Health works to improve the health and well-being of women and girls in the United States.

Facts and Illustrations

What Is Stress?

- According to a 2012 online survey conducted by Harris Interactive, on a scale of **1 to 10**, those in their late teens to early adulthood report a stress level of **5.4**, compared with **4.9** for older adults.

- In the APA's 2014 *Stress in America* study, twice as many teens said their stress increased over the previous year than teens who said their stress decreased.

- According to Richard Earle, a scientist who cofounded the Canadian Institute of Stress, people's stress levels go up and down hundreds of times each day.

- According the APA's 2014 *Stress in America* study, **37 percent** of teen girls feel sad or depressed, compared with **23 percent** of teen boys.

- In a 2012 study by researchers at the University of California–Los Angeles, black teenage girls reported feeling less stressed than white teenage girls.

- Mental health advocacy group Minding Your Mind states that adolescents with mental health disorders begin to show symptoms between **ages 14 and 24**.

- Market researcher Mike Hais suggests in a 2013 *USA Today* article that teens may be more willing to admit to being stressed than older people are.

Teens Stressed Beyond What Is Healthy

In February 2014 the American Psychological Association released a study showing how stress affects people in the United States. One finding (shown in this graph) is that teens' stress levels are higher than what teens themselves believe to be healthy. Study participants ranked their stress levels using a 10-point scale, with 1 indicating little or no stress and 10 indicating a great deal of stress. Twenty-seven percent of teens rated their school-year stress levels to be as high as 8, 9, or even 10, and 13 percent said they experience stress levels that high during the summer.

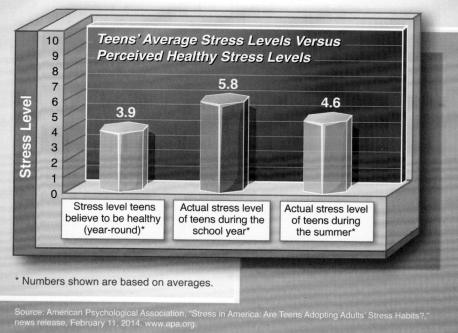

Teens' Average Stress Levels Versus Perceived Healthy Stress Levels

Stress Level

| Stress level teens believe to be healthy (year-round)* | Actual stress level of teens during the school year* | Actual stress level of teens during the summer* |
| 3.9 | 5.8 | 4.6 |

* Numbers shown are based on averages.

Source: American Psychological Association, "Stress in America: Are Teens Adopting Adults' Stress Habits?," news release, February 11, 2014. www.apa.org.

- The US Department of Education states that **50 percent** of youth with mental health disorders drop out of high school.

- According to the Johns Hopkins Bloomberg School of Public Health, teens experience a more rapid physical response to stress than adults because the prefrontal cortex, which assesses danger and triggers the stress response, is not fully developed in adolescents.

Teens' Stress Markedly Increases with Age

Research has shown that people of all ages suffer from stress overload. One study conducted by school officials in the Boston, Massachusetts, suburb of Wellesley found that stress levels are significantly higher among older students than younger students.

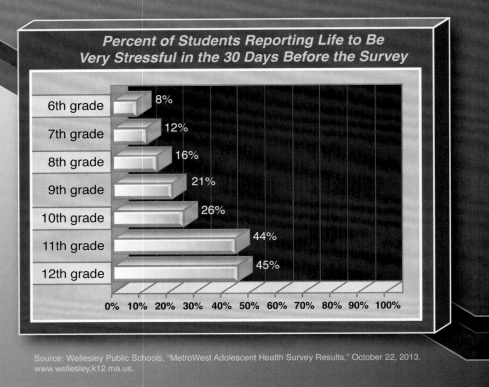

Percent of Students Reporting Life to Be Very Stressful in the 30 Days Before the Survey

Grade	Percent
6th grade	8%
7th grade	12%
8th grade	16%
9th grade	21%
10th grade	26%
11th grade	44%
12th grade	45%

Source: Wellesley Public Schools, "MetroWest Adolescent Health Survey Results," October 22, 2013. www.wellesley.k12.ma.us.

- According to the National Alliance on Mental Illness, **50 percent** of college students rate their mental health as "below average."

- According to the APA's 2014 *Stress in America* study, teens report higher stress levels than adults during the school year.

- The stress-related behaviors exhibited by adults—such as poor eating habits, lack of exercise, and lack of sleep—can be seen as early as the teen years, according to clinical psychologist Norman Anderson.

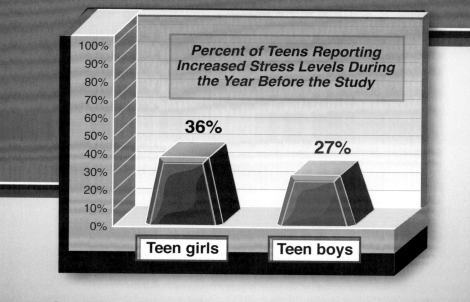

Teen Girls More Stressed-Out than Boys

Even though all teens experience stress, girls report higher levels of stress than boys. This is the finding of an American Psychological Association study released in February 2014.

Percent of Teens Reporting Increased Stress Levels During the Year Before the Study

36% — Teen girls

27% — Teen boys

Source: American Psychological Association, *Stress in America*, February 11, 2014. www.apa.org.

- A 2013 study by researchers from Stockholm, Sweden, found that **one-third** of all Swedish sixteen-year-olds are seriously stressed-out, with about **10 percent** of those teens also having symptoms of acute burnout.

- According to clinical psychologist and author Roni Cohen-Sandler, boys express stress more directly, whereas girls tend to keep their stress hidden.

What Causes Teens to Get Stressed?

66 **Some people are simply biologically prone to stress. Many outside factors influence susceptibility as well.** 99

—University of Maryland Medical Center, one of the oldest academic medical centers in the United States.

66 **Teens are dealing with multiple demands of school, peers and family. It's a lot of pressure.** 99

—Michelle Cutler, a clinical psychologist in Chicago, Illinois, who specializes in working with children and teens.

By the time Matt Lehrer was a junior in high school, he had grown frustrated with the continuous emphasis on college preparation. He felt like high school was enough to handle at that point in his life without constantly hearing about the importance of getting into a good college. Assemblies started during his freshman year to let students know what the school would be doing to help them prepare for college. "Sophomore year brought more assemblies," says Lehrer, "most of which reminded us to start thinking about college now."[41] Lehrer adds that school officials planned the assemblies to familiarize students with the college application process. But, as he explains, "they also succeeded in giving me panic attacks. They made it seem like colleges were watching my every move."[42]

This pressure about the importance of planning for his future was extremely stressful for Lehrer, so much so that he began to dread the thought of college rather than looking forward to it. "When I think about college I start to feel doomed," he says. "What if I can't get into a good college? Does that mean I won't get a good job? Am I going to be miserable for the rest of my life because I couldn't get an A?"[43]

Too Many Demands, Too Little Time

Lehrer says he was working as hard as he could on his schoolwork but still not measuring up to his parents' and teachers' expectations. "It makes me crazy," he says, "because I don't know what school I want to go to and hearing all the requirements confuses me even more. I have enough worries about my physics test next week." What was especially stressful for Lehrer was that he felt like he was supposed to fit into some kind of mold. "I get all panicky about getting into a 'good college' when I'm not even sure that's the right fit for me. What others might consider a good college might not fit in with my plans for the future."[44]

Many young people can identify with Lehrer's feelings. Although the specific causes of teen stress vary, specialists say that teens feel unable to cope with so many demands on their time. A teenage girl named Jan shares the various frustrations that stress her out:

> The worst thing about eleventh grade is the pressure to get into a good school. My parents are pushing me to study harder. Plus, you get pressured by all your friends to spend time with them, to go to their party or hang out. Have this boyfriend; you need one. Or you get stressed about homecoming. It's a big deal. Are you going? Who with? Do you have a dress? And with all this, I hope I get into a really good school and don't die from the stress of applying.[45]

Stressed-Out by School

One thing that was revealed in the APA's 2014 *Stress in America* study is that school-related stress is extremely common among teens. The study found that for 83 percent of teens, school is either somewhat a source of stress or a significant source of stress. Of those, using a 10-point scale, with 1 signifying no stress and 10 signifying extremely high stress, 27 percent of teens said they experienced stress at a level of 8, 9, or even 10 during the school year.

A smaller, localized study was conducted in Lyons Township, Illinois, which is close to Chicago. During the fall of 2013 Lyons Township school officials surveyed parents, teachers, and students. When asked whether academic stress was a problem, 75 percent of teachers said that it was, whereas 79 percent of students said they suffered from academic stress.

One Lyons Township High School student, Gillian Dunlop, shares her thoughts: "I think over five hours of homework a night is too much to put on a person and expect them to complete each assignment well. If you think about it, it's almost another full school day just in your home."[46] Because Dunlop is involved in extracurricular activities, it is not unusual for her to get home as late as 10:00 p.m. on school nights. Once she has spent the time necessary to complete her homework, she may only get about five hours of sleep—and sometimes not even that much. Like many of her classmates, Dunlop finds this rigorous schedule to be stressful.

> **Many of the same factors that cause stress for youth living in cities also cause stress for young people living in rural areas.**

A study published in September 2013 also focused on young people's school-related stress levels. The study was cosponsored by NPR, the Robert Wood Johnson Foundation, and the Harvard School of Public Health. It involved nearly fourteen hundred adults, including parents, stepparents, or guardians of children and teens (referred to as "parents" throughout the report). Participants were asked whether their child had been stressed during the past school year from a variety of potentially stressful school experiences. These included pressure to exceed academically, too much homework, bullying at school, difficult relationships with other students, difficult relationships with teachers, and violence or safety issues in school or somewhere in the surrounding neighborhood.

Among parents with children in grades six through eight, 36 percent said their child had experienced a lot of stress from at least one of the listed factors. The rate was slightly higher among parents with teens in grades nine through twelve; 38 percent said their child had experienced a lot of stress from at least one of the listed factors. Homework was found to be the leading source of stress, with 24 percent of parents saying their teenagers had experienced a lot of stress over the amount of homework they were assigned. Relationships with other students, violence and safety issues, and difficult relationships with teachers were also identified by parents as school-related stressors for their children.

Stress Among Rural Teens

Many of the same factors that cause stress for youth living in cities also cause stress for young people living in rural areas, although a study conducted in 2013 found some differences. Researchers from Mississippi State University and North Dakota State University published a study titled "Personal Problems Among Rural Youth and Their Relation to Psychosocial Well-Being." The researchers had observed that an abundance of research had been conducted on how stress affects adolescents, but it almost exclusively focused on youth in urban areas of the United States. "Despite the fact that approximately 25% of the nation's youth live in rural areas," the June 2013 report states, "where stress research is concerned, rural youth have been an understudied, neglected population."[47] The purpose of the 2013 study was to identify the types and frequencies of stressors experienced by teens living in rural areas, and then to evaluate the relationship between these stressors and the teens' well being.

Participants included ninety-nine adolescents (fifty-seven boys and forty-two girls), of various ethnicities and family types, who attend a rural high school in the southeastern United States. Each of the teens filled out a comprehensive questionnaire called the Personal Problems Checklist for Adolescents, which contained 240 questions about potential stressors. The questions were categorized into thirteen groups known as domains, which included appearance, attitude, crises, dating and sex, emotions, family, health, home, money, parents, religion, school, and social.

The study revealed that the main stressors for teens were in the social domain, with 80 percent reporting at least one problem in this area. The next-highest stressor was family, with 76 percent of teens citing this as a stressor; and closely behind that was the parents domain at 74 percent. Specific problems cited in the family and parents domains included not having any privacy at home, parents being too strict, parents disapproving of boyfriend or girlfriend, and arguing with brother or sister. Another finding was that teens living in stepfamilies reported more stress than those in intact families, meaning with biological parents. "In virtually every area of assessment," the report states, "stepchildren are found to fare more poorly, on average, than children living with both of their parents, although the differences are small." The researchers emphasize that even though these problems may seem minor when adults hear about them, "they nonetheless constitute very real sources of stress for the adolescent."[48]

The Relentless Stress of Being Bullied

According to the federal antibullying agency StopBullying.gov, 28 percent of students in the United States in sixth through twelfth grades have experienced bullying. Data compiled by the agency also show that sometime in the preceding year, 6 percent of students in grades six through twelve have been cyberbullied. When evaluating high school alone, the rate more than doubles to 16 percent of students. Of parents who participated in the 2013 NPR/ Robert Wood Johnson Foundation/ Harvard School of Public Health survey, 40 percent said that bullying caused stress for their children. "One of the most painful aspects of bullying is that it is relentless," says the Nemours Foundation. "Most people can take one episode of teasing or name calling or being shunned at the mall. However, when it goes on and on, bullying can put a person in a state of constant fear."[49]

> According to the federal antibullying agency StopBullying.gov, 28 percent of students in the United States in sixth through twelfth grades have experienced bullying.

Nemours goes on to say that young people who are abused by their peers are at risk for a number of mental health problems, including low self-esteem, depression, and anxiety, as well as severe stress. One example is a teenage girl named Amber, who "began having stomach pains and diarrhea and was diagnosed with a digestive condition called irritable bowel syndrome as a result of the stress that came from being bullied throughout ninth grade." Another teenager, a boy named Mahfooz, "spent his afternoons hungry and unable to concentrate in class because he was too afraid to go to the school cafeteria at lunchtime."[50]

One school district where bullying and cyberbullying have been identified as serious stressors for students is in Wellesley, Massachusetts. In October 2013 school officials released the MetroWest Adolescent Health Survey, which involved middle school and high school students. The survey showed that 14 percent of middle schoolers and 33 percent of high schoolers were finding life to be "very stressful" in the thirty-day period preceding the study. When asked about bullying during that period, 41 percent of middle schoolers said they had been bullied and 17 percent had been cyberbullied. Among high school students, 27 percent reported being bullied in the past thirty days and 22 percent had been cyberbullied. Says high school wellness teacher Bruce Elliott, "Stress levels for students are going up and up and up and up."[51]

Less Sleep Equals More Stress

The National Sleep Foundation says that teenagers need nine to nine and one-quarter hours of sleep each night—but only a fraction of them get that much sleep. This is a vicious cycle: Stress has an impact on teens' sleep, and teens' lack of sleep has an impact on their stress levels. Social psychologist and renowned sleep expert James Maas says that most high school students get two and a half fewer hours of sleep per night than they need. "Every single high school student I have ever measured in terms of their alertness is a walking zombie,"[52] says Maas.

For a study published in the November 2013 issue of the *Journal of Adolescent Health*, University of California–Berkeley researcher Lauren D. Asarnow and colleagues compared the various sleep habits of a large group of teens aged thirteen to eighteen. The goal of the study was to determine the significance of late bedtimes,

> " The National Sleep Foundation says that teenagers need nine to nine and one-quarter hours of sleep each night—but only a fraction of them get that much sleep. "

> **Just as no two teenagers are exactly the same, the causes of their stress are different as well.**

sleep duration, and sleep constrained by early school start times on young people's social and emotional development. Asarnow's group found that teens who stay up past 11:30 p.m. on school nights—nearly one-third of the teens analyzed in the study—are more likely to have academic and emotional difficulties throughout high school and beyond. Says psychologist Allison Harvey, who was senior author of the paper, "This very important study adds to the already clear evidence that youth who are night owls are at greater risk for adverse outcomes. Helping teens go to bed earlier may be an important pathway for reducing risk."[53]

Complexities Abound

Just as no two teenagers are exactly the same, the causes of their stress are different as well. Studies have revealed a number of common stressors, however, including school-related pressure, difficulties within the family, bullying and cyberbullying, and insufficient amounts of sleep. As research progresses and awareness that teen stress is a real problem continues to grow, this may lead to better stress management strategies to help young people cope with stress before it becomes overwhelming.

What Causes Teens to Get Stressed?

❝Family relationships can be very stressful, but friend-ships are often under rated for the stress they cause, especially when jealousy and misunderstandings take place.❞

—Janet Matthews, *Is Stress Your Silent Killer?*, Hereford, UK: Your Healthy Options, 2012, p. 10.

Matthews is a nutritionist and retired head teacher at a school in England for young people with emotional and behavioral problems.

....

❝Children from lower-income homes tend to have higher levels of stress hormones than their higher-income peers.❞

—Wayne Weiten, Dana S. Dunn, and Elizabeth Yost Hammer, *Psychology Applied to Modern Life*. Stamford, CT: Cengage Learning, 2013, p. 70.

Weiten, Dunn, and Hammer are psychologists.

....

* Editor's Note: While the definition of a primary source can be narrowly or broadly defined, for the purposes of Compact Research, a primary source consists of: 1) results of original research presented by an organization or researcher; 2) eyewitness accounts of events, personal experience, or work experience; 3) first-person editorials offering pundits' opinions; 4) government officials presenting political plans and/or policies; 5) representatives of organizations presenting testimony or policy.

> **Pressure to excel at home, school, sports, and extra-curricular activities creates a constant high-stress environment with no downtime.**

—Lori Lite, *Stress Free Kids*. Avon, MA: Adams Media, 2014, p. 12.

Lite is a certified children's meditation facilitator, author, and founder of the Marietta, Georgia–based group Stress Free Kids.

> **When it comes to stress, teens who get fewer than eight hours of sleep on a school night appear to fare worse than teens getting eight hours of sleep on school nights.**

—American Psychological Association, *Stress in America: Are Teens Adopting Adults' Stress Habits?*, February 11, 2014. www.apa.org.

The APA is America's largest scientific and professional organization representing the field of psychology.

> **There seems to be an increase in adolescent stress. We think this is due to a combination of increasing stressors and decreased coping skills.**

—Henri Roca, interviewed by two high school students, "Teen Stress—an Interview," Dr. Henri Roca, February 13, 2013. http://drhenriroca.com.

Roca is a family medicine physician from Greenwich, Connecticut.

> **Almost anything can cause stress and it has different triggers.**

—Christian Nordqvist, "What Is Stress? How to Deal with Stress," Medical News Today, July 30, 2014. www.medicalnewstoday.com.

Nordqvist is cofounder and editor of Medical News Today.

❝Competition, after school activities, a lack of sleep, a crunched schedule, peer pressure, tests, and bullying are just a few things that boost our kids unhealthy stress levels.❞

—Michele Borba, "Signs of Stress in Kids and Teens and How to Reduce It," *Dr. Michele Borba* (blog), December 8, 2013. http://micheleborba.com.

Borba is an educational consultant who holds a doctorate in educational psychology and counseling.

❝The teen years often bring about an increase in perceived stress as young adults learn to cope with increasing demands and pressures along with changes in their bodies.❞

—Melissa Conrad Stöppler, "Stress," MedicineNet, September 4, 2013. www.medicinenet.com.

Stöppler is a physician and medical journalist.

What Causes Teens to Get Stressed?

- In the APA's 2014 *Stress in America* study, more than half of teens reported that time management is a significant stressor.

- According to the mental health advocacy group Minding Your Mind, sources of stress among adolescents today include the volatile economy, the increased costs of higher education, and the increased cost of living.

- The Internet and other modern technology contribute to adolescents feeling disconnected and anxious, which leads to a general sense of meaninglessness and despair, according to Allen O'Barr, director of counseling and wellness services at the University of North Carolina–Chapel Hill.

- According to the 2014 *Teens Take on Health* report, sponsored by the National 4-H Council and Molina Healthcare, **18 percent** of teens say that they are more stressed when they do not get enough sleep.

- In a 2012 online survey by Harris Interactive, **76 percent** of respondents aged **18 to 33** cited work as a chief source of stress, and another **73 percent** cited money.

- Market researcher Mike Hais suggests in a 2013 *USA Today* article that higher stress levels in teens are due to a combination of their life phase and the fact that the economy took a downturn right as many came of age.

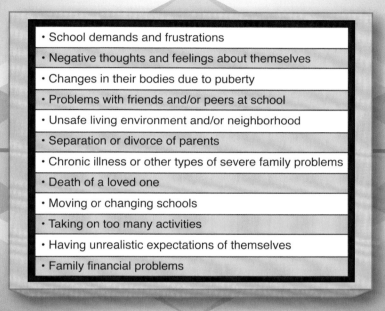

Numerous Reasons for Stress Overload

Adolescence can be a challenging time, and teens often feel overwhelmed by pressure caused by school, family, relationships, and other factors. Shown here are some of the main sources of stress for young people.

- School demands and frustrations
- Negative thoughts and feelings about themselves
- Changes in their bodies due to puberty
- Problems with friends and/or peers at school
- Unsafe living environment and/or neighborhood
- Separation or divorce of parents
- Chronic illness or other types of severe family problems
- Death of a loved one
- Moving or changing schools
- Taking on too many activities
- Having unrealistic expectations of themselves
- Family financial problems

Source: American Academy of Child & Adolescent Psychiatry, "Helping Teenagers Deal with Stress," *Facts for Families*, February 2013. www.aacap.org.

- The bleak job market is a large source of stress for young people; as of January 2013 the unemployment rate for those aged **18 to 29** was **13 percent**, according to *USA Today*.

- Teens who reported high stress levels in the APA's 2014 *Stress in America* study spend an average of **3.2 hours** online each day, whereas low-stress teens spend an average of **2 hours** online each day.

Stressed-Out by Cruelty

Studies have shown that young people who experience bullying and cyberbullying also experience a great deal of stress as they try to cope with this treatment day after day. A 2013 study conducted by researchers from the Urban Institute Justice Policy Center found that young people who are cyberbullied have a higher incidence* of depression, anger/hostility, and anxiety than those who are not victims of cyberbullying.

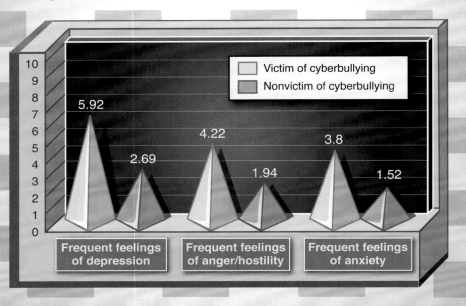

*Note: The higher the number, the greater frequency of depression, anger/hostility, and anxiety among teens surveyed.

Source: Janine M. Zweig et al., "Technology, Teen Dating Violence and Abuse, and Bullying," Urban Institute Justice Policy Center, July 2013. www.ncjrs.gov.

- Today's high school students cite worries about the future—including student loan debt, finding a job, and struggling to reach the same standard of living as their parents—as major stressors, according to a 2014 H&R Block survey of **1,000 13- to 17-year-olds**.

- The National Child Traumatic Stress Network suggests that keeping up with news about the economy can cause a teen to dwell on the future and become more stressed.

Teens Cite School as Biggest Source of Stress

To determine what teens find most stressful in their lives, the Palo Alto Medical Foundation surveyed 124 adolescents in 2013. Those who took part in the survey identified homework and school as the biggest sources of stress in their lives.

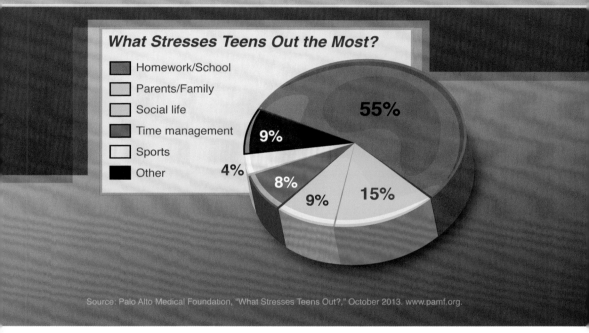

What Stresses Teens Out the Most?

- Homework/School
- Parents/Family
- Social life
- Time management
- Sports
- Other

55%
9%
4%
8%
9%
15%

Source: Palo Alto Medical Foundation, "What Stresses Teens Out?," October 2013. www.pamf.org.

- According to the Johns Hopkins Bloomberg School of Public Health, social pressure to be a particular size or shape is a major stressor for teens; for girls the focus is on being thin, whereas for boys it is on having an athletic physique.

- In a 2014 survey of **124 adolescents** conducted by the Palo Alto Medical Foundation, **55 percent** said their top stressors were grades, tests, getting into college, and finals week.

What Health Problems Are Associated with Stress?

❝Stress is the silent killer.❞

—Terry Gordon, a retired cardiologist and the author of *No Storm Lasts Forever: Transforming Suffering into Insight*.

❝When stress builds up and isn't dealt with in a healthy way, it can diminish a person's energy, compromise the immune system, and lead to anxiety problems.❞

—Massachusetts Medical Society Alliance, which advocates and promotes good health among the citizens of Massachusetts.

When young people get overloaded with stress, they become vulnerable to numerous health problems. One of the most common ailments associated with stress is headaches; nearly one-third of teens who participated in the APA *Stress in America* survey said that they suffer from headaches because of stress. This is not unusual, as San Francisco pediatrician Charles J. Wibbelsman explains: "The most common adolescent headaches are tension headaches, specifically related to stresses in their lives—school, exams, sports, and extracurricular activities." It is telling, says Wibbelsman, that "many tension headaches go away in the summer, when school's out."[54]

Colleen Frainey suffered from frequent nagging headaches, as well as stomachaches, during a time in her life that was very stressful. When the Tualatin, Oregon, teenager was a sophomore in high school, she was taking all advanced courses, and the pressure of the workload was just too much. "I didn't feel good," she says, "and when I didn't feel good I felt like I couldn't do my work, which would stress me out more."[55] Frainey and her parents knew that something had to change—her health and well-being depended on it. So she dropped one of her advanced courses to make her schedule more manageable, and this alone improved her quality of life. She had more time to spend with her family and friends, as well as to care for and ride her beloved horse, Bishop. Before long her health was back to normal, too, and she was no longer troubled by headaches and stomachaches.

Stress and the Immune System

Scientists have known about the close association between stress and human illness since the 1980s, when several researchers began to focus on it. Studies have shown that poor health is more common among people with high-stress lives because stress weakens the immune system, which is the body's main defense against infection and disease. British researcher Saul McLeod explains: "The immune system is a collection of billions of cells that travel through the bloodstream. They move in and out of tissues and organs, defending the body against foreign bodies (antigens), such as bacteria, viruses and cancerous cells." When the body is stressed, this reduces the immune system's ability to fight off antigens, says McLeod, which is why people are more vulnerable to infection and disease when they are overloaded with stress. "Stress can also have an indirect effect on the immune system," he adds, "as a person may use unhealthy behavioral coping strategies to reduce their stress, such as drinking and smoking."[56]

> **One of the most common ailments associated with stress is headaches.**

The fact that stress impairs immune system function helps explain why teens who are under a great deal of stress get sick with colds more often than those who are not as stressed. Scientists have been aware of this connection for years, but they remained puzzled about exactly how stress influences immunity. A study published in April 2012 helped shed light on the scientific uncertainty. The research team that performed the study was led by Sheldon Cohen, a professor of psychology and renowned stress researcher at Carnegie Mellon University in Pittsburgh, Pennsylvania. The study revealed that when someone suffers from chronic stress, the body can lose its natural ability to regulate an immune reaction called the inflammatory response. Creating inflammation is the body's way of protecting against infection and disease, and its purpose is to destroy harmful antigens that can cause disease. The inflammatory response causes symptoms that are often confused with symptoms of infection, as Cohen explains: "The symptoms of a cold are not caused directly by the virus, they're caused by the inflammatory response to the infection. You want to produce enough of inflammation to fight off the infection, but not so much that you experience cold symptoms."[57]

> "When someone suffers from chronic stress, the body can lose its natural ability to regulate an immune reaction called the inflammatory response.

Cohen's study involved two separate experiments. In the first, researchers interviewed 276 healthy adult volunteers and asked questions about what had caused the most stress in their lives during the past year. All participants were then exposed to a common cold virus by having it dripped into their noses. For the next five days they were quarantined and monitored for signs of infection and illness. When the five-day period was over, 39 percent of the participants had gotten sick with a cold. In confirmation of Cohen's theory about stress and the immune system, participants who had experienced the greatest amount of stress in their lives were sick at twice the rate of the others.

The second part of the study involved seventy-nine healthy participants and confirmed that the immune system's inflammatory response was impaired by stress. Specifically, the researchers found that when the participants were suffering from high stress, their bodies produced too much of the stress hormone cortisol, which serves as an on/off switch for the inflammatory response. Too much cortisol causes too much inflammation by upsetting the immune system's normal balance, which ultimately leads to the development of a full-blown cold. "Inflammation is partly regulated by the hormone cortisol," says Cohen, "and when cortisol is not allowed to serve this function, inflammation can get out of control."[58] He goes on to say that this finding could play a critical role in identifying other diseases that may be influenced by stress, as well as preventing disease in people who suffer from chronic stress.

Beyond Stomachaches

Among the most common ailments to affect teens who suffer from stress overload are digestive problems. "When you're stressed," says the APA, "your brain becomes more alert to sensations in your stomach. Your stomach can react with 'butterflies' or even nausea or pain. You may vomit if the stress is severe enough. And, if the stress becomes chronic, you may develop ulcers or severe stomach pain even without ulcers."[59] Teens with high stress levels may suffer from heartburn or acid reflux, a condition in which digestive acids flow back up into the esophagus from the stomach. "Stress or exhaustion can also increase the severity of heartburn pain,"[60] says the APA. Diarrhea and constipation are also common among high-stress teens, as are gas pains and bloating.

A stress-related digestive disorder that can be especially hard for teens to cope with is irritable bowel syndrome (IBS), which was formerly called spastic colon. The Nemours Foundation describes the syndrome as a "somewhat baffling yet common intestinal disorder that affects the colon (the large intestine.)"[61] Nemours goes on to explain that the colon's primary function is to absorb water and nutrients from partially digested food. Whatever is not absorbed moves through the colon toward the rectum and out of the body in the form of feces, or waste material. This digestive process works with the help of smooth, wave-like muscle contractions; for someone with IBS, however, the muscles do not work properly. "When this happens," says the Nemours Foundation, "a person can feel the abdominal cramps,

> **Teens with high stress levels may suffer from heartburn or acid reflux, a condition in which digestive acids flow back up into the esophagus from the stomach.**

bloating, constipation, and diarrhea that may be signs of IBS."[62]

One teenager who knows from personal experience how difficult it is to live with IBS is a girl named Nicolle. She was diagnosed when she was a sophomore in high school after experiencing symptoms such as severe diarrhea; she says, "Everything I ate would usually go right through me."[63] Nicolle also suffered from constipation, bloating, and abdominal cramps so painful that she has difficulty describing them. Because she suffers from high stress and anxiety, she says this makes her condition worse. Having to cope with IBS day after day is very frustrating for her.

In May 2012 Nicolle wrote in an online forum about the many difficulties of living with the condition. "Every day is a constant struggle with IBS," she says. Formerly an A student, Nicolle often makes excuses not to go to school out of fear that she will have an attack of severe abdominal cramps followed by diarrhea. When she is at school, she rarely eats anything in an effort to avoid a flare-up. "In other words," she writes, "I'm afraid that if I eat, my IBS will act up and I'll be stranded in an awfully uncomfortable situation." Nicolle hopes that she does not have to live with IBS for the rest of her life, because she cannot imagine that, nor does she want anyone else to be afflicted by it. "I just wish this would go away and no one would have to suffer from it,"[64] she says.

From Stressed to Depressed

In addition to digestive ailments, chronic stress has also been linked to depression, which is a serious condition that causes persistent feelings of sadness and despair, often accompanied by a loss of interest in activities the person once enjoyed. The Mayo Clinic says that depression affects how teens think, feel, and behave, "and it can cause emotional, functional and physical problems."[65] Although teens who are feeling sad or down may say that they are depressed, the disease of depression goes much deeper than that. Hopelessness and despair are common among depressed teens, as is suicidal thinking and behavior.

Scientists do not know exactly what causes depression, but they believe that a number of factors are involved, including genetics, biology, personality type, environment—and stress. Although much is still unknown about the link between stress and depression, research has yielded a number of promising clues. One theory, which resulted from a 2012 study published in the medical journal *Biological Psychiatry*, is that chronic stress can actually shrink gray matter (tissue containing nerve cell bodies and their branches, known as dendrites) in the prefrontal cortex. This is the part of the brain that is critical for regulation of emotions; desires, impulses, and self-control; and physiological functions such as blood pressure and glucose levels. "The brain is dynamic and plastic," says Rajita Sinha, professor in Yale University's Department of Neurobiology, "and things can improve—but only if stress is dealt with in a healthy manner. If not, the effects of stress can have a negative impact on both our physical and mental health."[66]

In 2013 researchers from Johns Hopkins School of Medicine released a study that helped explain the link between stress in teens and the development of depression later in life. Working with mice that were bred to have genes for mental illness, researchers were able to trigger signs and symptoms of depression and other disorders by putting the mice in situations that caused them stress. "Having the genes for mental illness puts the mice at risk," says Akira Sawa, a psychiatry professor and director of the schizophrenia center at Johns Hopkins Medical Center and lead researcher on the study, "but it

> **Although much is still unknown about the link between stress and depression, research has yielded a number of promising clues.**

is not enough to cause mental illness. When you add stress to the equation, at an age when the mouse brain is most similar to the human adolescent brain, the mental illness is triggered."[67]

The researchers induced stress in the mice by isolating those that were genetically bred for mental illness from the other mice. This isolation of the genetically altered mice caused their brains to release cortisol, which in turn affected levels of another brain chemical known as dopamine. This was a profound discovery because changes in dopamine have been implicated in several mental illnesses, including schizophrenia, bipolar disorder, and depression, among others. "I think most clinicians would agree that adolescent stress can cause major changes in adult brains," says Sawa. "The adolescent brain is at a unique stage of development. It is a time when the brain is very sensitive and in the process of forming its wiring network."[68] Sawa goes on to explain that adolescent brains may be more sensitive to cortisol and may feel its effects more quickly than adult brains. Because the brain's prefrontal cortex, which is responsible for shutting down the stress response, is less developed in adolescents, they may experience stress for longer periods of time, including into their adult years.

From Difficult to Dangerous

From headaches to colds, digestive disorders, immune system impairment, and mental illness, stress can definitely be harmful to health. For many years scientists knew this but found it challenging to prove exactly how stress was linked to illness. Through studies by renowned stress researchers and their colleagues, many questions have been answered. Still, however, there is work to be done because much about the relationship between stress in teens and illness remains unknown.

Primary Source Quotes*

What Health Problems Are Associated with Stress?

66 **Just about every bodily system or body part is affected by stress.** 99

—Allen Elkin, *Stress Management for Dummies*. Hoboken, NJ: Wiley, 2013, p. 16.

Elkin is a clinical psychologist who practices in New York City.

66 **Studies have shown that excessive stress during the teen years can have a negative impact upon both physical and mental health later in life.** 99

—Melissa Conrad Stöppler, "Stress," MedicineNet, September 4, 2013. www.medicinenet.com.

Stöppler is a physician and medical journalist.

66 **The experience of stress, particularly chronic stress, takes a significant toll on the well-being of individuals in terms of emotional and physical discomforts as well as functional ability.** 99

—Brenda L. Lyon, "Stress, Coping, and Health," in *Handbook of Stress, Coping, and Health: Implications for Nursing Research*, ed. Virginia Hill Rice. Thousand Oaks, CA: Sage, 2012, p. 3.

Lyon holds a PhD in nursing from Indiana University and has specialized in stress and stress management for nearly forty years.

* Editor's Note: While the definition of a primary source can be narrowly or broadly defined, for the purposes of Compact Research, a primary source consists of: 1) results of original research presented by an organization or researcher; 2) eyewitness accounts of events, personal experience, or work experience; 3) first-person editorials offering pundits' opinions; 4) government officials presenting political plans and/or policies; 5) representatives of organizations presenting testimony or policy.

❝Chronic stress symptoms break down children's immune system as well as increasing their likelihood for depression.❞

—Michele Borba, "Signs of Stress in Kids and Teens and How to Reduce It," *Dr. Michele Borba* (blog), December 8, 2013. http://micheleborba.com.

Borba is an educational consultant who holds a doctorate in educational psychology and counseling.

❝A persistently negative response to challenges will eventually have a negative effect on your health and happiness.❞

—Christian Nordqvist, "What Is Stress? How to Deal with Stress," Medical News Today, July 30, 2014. www.medicalnewstoday.com.

Nordqvist is cofounder and editor of Medical News Today.

❝Stress symptoms may be affecting your health, even though you might not realize it.❞

—Mayo Clinic, "Stress Management," July 19, 2013. www.mayoclinic.org.

The Mayo Clinic is a world-renowned health care facility headquartered in Rochester, Minnesota.

❝Struggling with major stress and low self-esteem issues can play a role in more serious problems such as eating disorders, hurting yourself, depression, alcohol and drug abuse, and even suicide.❞

—Office on Women's Health, "Feeling Stressed," April 9, 2014. http://girlshealth.gov.

The Office on Women's Health works to improve the health and well-being of women and girls in the United States.

"Poverty-related stress takes its toll on both physical and mental health."

—Wayne Weiten, Dana S. Dunn, and Elizabeth Yost Hammer, *Psychology Applied to Modern Life*. Stamford, CT: Cengage Learning, 2013, p. 70.

Weiten, Dunn, and Hammer are psychologists.

"Stress reduces quality of life by affecting feelings of pleasure and accomplishment."

—University of Maryland Medical Center, "Stress," June 26, 2013. http://umm.edu.

Located in downtown Baltimore, the University of Maryland Medical Center is one of the oldest academic medical centers in the United States.

Facts and Illustrations

What Health Problems Are Associated with Stress?

- The APA's 2014 *Stress in America* study found that stress leads to a number of health issues for teens: **One-third** experienced headaches, **one-fourth** experienced a change in sleeping habits, and just over **one-fifth** experienced stomach or digestive problems.

- According to the National Alliance on Mental Illness, stress is a major contributor to teen depression, and about **1 in 5 teens** will experience depression at some point.

- A 2012 study by researchers at the University of California–Los Angeles found that although stressed-out black teenage girls and white teenage girls both tend to gain weight, stress appears to have a greater effect on the weight of black girls.

- Depression and anxiety are the most common mental health problems for college students, and suicide is the second leading cause of death (after accidents) among college students, accounting for **1,100 deaths** per year, according to John MacPhee, executive director of the Jed Foundation.

- According to the APA's 2014 *Stress in America* study, **36 percent** of teens report feeling tired due to stress.

- The teen advocacy website TeenHelp.com estimates that **10 percent** of teens suffer from an anxiety disorder.

A Multitude of Problems

Stress is a normal part of daily life, but teens who suffer from high levels of stress over a long period of time can develop health problems. According to the Mayo Clinic, these problems can range from headaches and muscle tension to anxiety, depression, and high blood pressure and other, more serious diseases.

Effects of Stress . . .

On the body	On mood	On behavior
Headache	Anxiety	Overeating or undereating
Muscle tension or pain	Restlessness	Angry outbursts
Chest pain	Lack of motivation or focus	Drug or alcohol abuse
Fatigue	Irritability or anger	Tobacco use
Upset stomach	Sadness or depression	Social withdrawal
Sleep problems		
If unchecked, stress can contribute to conditions such as high blood pressure, heart disease, obesity, and diabetes		

Source: Mayo Clinic, "Stress Management," July 19, 2013. www.mayoclinic.org.

- According to a 2013 Harris Interactive survey conducted for Teen Line, a hotline at Cedars-Sinai Medical Center in Los Angeles, **54 percent** of teens believe that their stress has little or no impact on their physical health, and **52 percent** believe it has little or no effect on their mental health.

- A 2012 study by researchers at the University of California–Los Angeles suggests that black teenage girls may produce more of the stress hormone cortisol than white teenage girls do, which could contribute to the disparity in obesity rates between black and white teenage girls.

Teens Troubled by Health Issues

During the American Psychological Association's most recent *Stress in America* survey, teens were asked about the effects of stress over the prior month. As shown here, they reported many problems related to their health and well-being.

Teens Reporting Stress-Related Problems in the Past Month

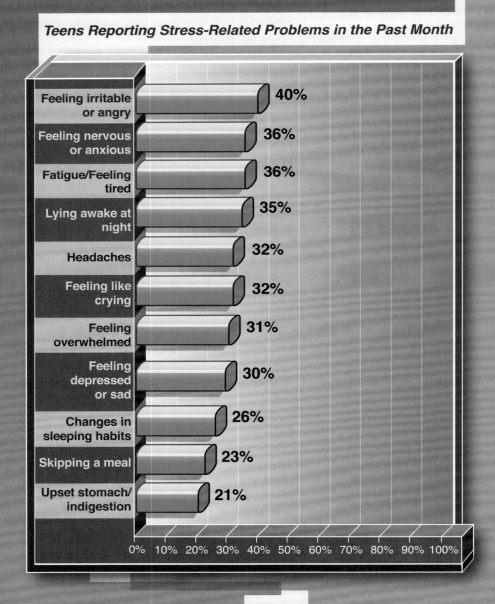

Problem	Percentage
Feeling irritable or angry	40%
Feeling nervous or anxious	36%
Fatigue/Feeling tired	36%
Lying awake at night	35%
Headaches	32%
Feeling like crying	32%
Feeling overwhelmed	31%
Feeling depressed or sad	30%
Changes in sleeping habits	26%
Skipping a meal	23%
Upset stomach/indigestion	21%

Source: American Psychological Association, *Stress in America: Are Teens Adopting Adults' Stress Habits?*, February 11, 2014. www.apa.org.

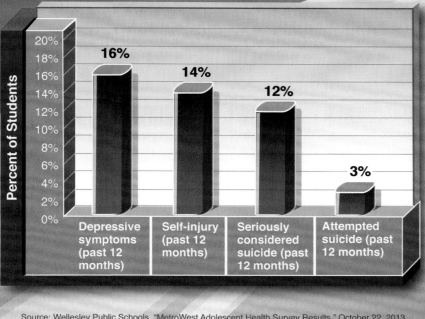

Stress Can Be Dangerous

Teens who are under a great deal of stress are at risk for many health problems; high stress has been linked to depression, self-injurious behavior (such as cutting), and suicide. One area of the country where school officials have identified teen stress as an issue of concern is the Boston, Massachusetts, suburb of Wellesley. This graph shows the percentages of health problems resulting from stress, based on the Wellesley school district's student survey.

Source: Wellesley Public Schools, "MetroWest Adolescent Health Survey Results," October 22, 2013. www.wellesley.k12.ma.us.

- Adolescents with mental health problems are **50 percent** more likely than adolescents without mental health problems to smoke and use illegal drugs, according to the mental health advocacy group Minding Your Mind.

- Long-term stressors such as coping with parental divorce or being bullied at school can weaken teens' immune systems and make them feel depleted of energy, according to the Johns Hopkins Bloomberg School of Public Health.

How Can Teens Cope with Stress?

❝We can't rid our lives of stress, but we all can learn how to cope with it.❞

—Palo Alto Medical Foundation, a health care organization headquartered in Palo Alto, California.

❝We won't find the future we have in mind if we just stop searching, working, altogether. But if we calm down and look around, we just might find something better.❞

—Lana Gorlinski, a teenage girl from Orange County, California.

In a February 2013 interview, New Orleans, Louisiana, physician Henri Roca responded to a number of questions about teen stress. When asked about some methods of coping with stress, Roca said there were three components to this: redefining the circumstances so they are no longer stressful; exercising to work stress out of the body; and adopting stress management skills. The first component involves changing one's self-expectations from perfection to doing the best one can. Roca offers encouragement, as well as a dose of common sense, for today's teens. "By the way, it's okay to not have your entire life planned out at this stage," he says. "The only way we grow is through trial and error. Perfectionists rarely grow because they rarely allow themselves to fail. Very often when they fail, they fall apart because they have no way of coping with anything less than perfection."[69]

Peace and Serenity

One of the points Roca made clear during his interview was that stress overload can absolutely be avoided. "No one and nothing can make you feel stressed," he says. "Stress is our natural response to our interpretation of the world. We are hard wired to avoid what we think will kill us. Now we spend a lot of time defining harmless things as things that will threaten our existence. Changing how we think is our best protection from stress. The best second option is to enhance the ability to be relaxed." Roca goes on to explain how teens might achieve this goal. "Participate in activities that are meaningful to you," he says. "Stress arises not from overscheduling overall, but rather from overscheduling things that are perceived as something you *should* do rather than things you *want* to do."[70]

One of Roca's recommendations is yoga, which has been shown to help reduce stress in people of all ages. Yoga allows teens to exercise in a noncompetitive environment, which helps them feel more confident and sure of themselves. The numerous benefits of yoga were revealed in a 2013 Harvard Medical School study. The researchers found that teens who practice yoga two to three times a week for ten weeks have significant improvement in mood, attitude, and overall stress levels. "There is something more that yoga provides beyond just physical fitness," says Carlos Santo, a holistic medical practitioner, acupuncturist, and yoga instructor from Phoenix, Arizona. "We have yet to measure it scientifically, but just because we can't measure it doesn't invalidate it."[71] Santo goes on to say that when people practice yoga, they are in tune with their bodies at all times. They learn to be aware of the breath and body, which helps normalize brain chemistry and helps them avoid getting overloaded with stress.

> " The researchers found that teens who practice yoga two to three times a week for ten weeks have significant improvement in mood, attitude, and overall stress levels. "

Eighteen-year-old Savannah Rossi lives in Phoenix and regularly practices yoga. Through her involvement in yoga Rossi feels she has become a more optimistic and positive person. She gets along better with her parents and other people than she did before she started practicing yoga, and a huge benefit is that she has learned to let go of stress. This has also been the experience of eighteen-year-old Phoenix resident Sydney

Reed. She has found that yoga helps her handle the stress that comes along with homework and tests. "Yoga helps me . . . calm down from the day so I can approach my studying with a clear mind," she says. "Yoga has taught me to focus on what I'm doing in the moment and not to worry so much."[72]

Crystal Woodward is a yoga instructor who holds classes designed especially for young people. She is convinced that yoga helps teens cope with the many stressors in their lives due to academic pressure, social issues, and poor self-confidence, as well as the normal emotional and hormonal changes that are characteristic of the teenage years. According to Woodward, mental and emotional benefits of yoga include improvements in mood and attitude, lower stress levels, and a sense of peace and calm, which helps teens feel more grounded and focused. "You see your students learn to breathe, relax and let go,"[73] she says.

Invaluable Benefits of Exercise

It is no secret that exercise can benefit people of all ages by helping them become physically fit and less vulnerable to disease. But exercise offers tremendous psychological benefits as well. In a 2013 paper published in the medical journal *JAMA Pediatrics*, the authors discuss the emotional benefits of exercise for young people. "Exercise is considered an active strategy to prevent and treat depression and anxiety for school-aged youth," they write. "It has been shown to promote positive thoughts and feelings, enhance confidence to cope with problems, and provide increased confidence and self-control. Participating in physical activity can also improve self-esteem and foster positive self-worth."[74]

Also in 2013, a team of researchers led by Catherine M. Sabiston, associate professor of kinesiology and physical education at McGill University in Montreal, Canada, published a study that examined how sports participation can help reduce stress in depression-prone teens. The study involved 1,293 Canadian adolescents from urban, suburban, and rural areas, of whom 52 percent were girls and 48 percent were boys. Over a period of five years, the teens completed surveys every three months about their mental health and their level of physical activity. Of the total participants in the study, 860 teens reported that they were involved in moderate to vigorous physical activity. Of those active young people, 41 percent had the lowest number of depressive symptoms of all participants, and 55.7 percent scored only slightly higher than that. The researchers were able to conclude that the more physically active teens were, the better they felt emotionally and the lower their risk for high stress and depression.

In 2014 a young Canadian woman named Adela Han wrote about how exercise had helped her sister, who had been struggling with depression. While in middle school the girl became so overloaded with schoolwork, relationship issues, extracurricular activities, and social status issues that she became overwhelmed by stress and started showing depressive symptoms. "She lost [her] appetite," says Han, "cried a lot, and seemed sad all the time." Han adds that she and her parents tried to help her sister, but she would not open up to them and talk about her problems. Then she started high school and joined the track team, which required regular workouts—and the difference was amazing. "She gradually became happier," says Han, "and her depressive symptoms decreased. In less than a year, she became a completely different person than when she was suffering from depression."[75]

> " The researchers were able to conclude that the more physically active teens were, the better they felt emotionally and the lower their risk for high stress and depression. "

Dancing Away the Stress

For various reasons many young people are not interested in joining school teams, and they may not know of or be interested in other opportunities to get regular exercise. Motivating teenage girls to learn how enjoyable exercise can be was the focus of a study published in 2013 by researchers from Sweden. The type of exercise they suggested to the girls was dance, as the report authors write: "Dance is a well-established and popular form of physical activity, particularly for young women. It can provide a supportive environment and an opportunity to enhance low body attitudes and physical self-perceptions. It is suggested that dance can reduce disabling conditions resulting from stress."[76]

The study involved a group of Swedish girls aged thirteen to eighteen who were all suffering from severe stress. Fifty-nine girls participated in the dance-exercise group and were known as the intervention group, while the others did not participate in the dance exercise. Those in the intervention group attended dance classes twice weekly for eight months. Each class lasted seventy-five minutes, and the focus was on the joy of movement, rather than on the skill of performance. At the end of the eight months, the girls who participated in dance reported improved emotional and physical health compared with the girls in the control group. Even four and eight months after the study ended, the girls who were part of the dance group were still experiencing a more positive outlook and lower stress levels. The report authors write:

> This study points out the role of joyful social physical activity in influencing health. We conclude that an intervention with dance twice weekly for 8 months is feasible and can improve [self-rated health] in adolescent girls with internalizing problems, even if the girls lacked previous experience in dancing. According to these results, despite problems such as stress and psychosomatic symptoms (and other potential challenges in being an adolescent girl), dance can result in high adherence and a positive experience for the participants, which might contribute to sustained new healthy habits.[77]

The Healing Power of Writing

When young people are troubled, including suffering from problems at home, at school, in relationships, or just life in general, mental health professionals often encourage them to keep a journal. Writing about what they are going through allows teens to get their feelings out, which is much healthier than keeping them inside where they end up growing and festering. "Research has shown that writing a personal diary and other forms of expressive writing are a great way to release emotional distress and just feel better," says Meyran Boniel-Nissim, a psychologist with the University of Haifa in Israel.[78]

In 2012 Boniel-Nissim led a team of researchers in conducting a study to determine whether blogging would help teens who were struggling with high stress and emotional issues. The study involved 161 teenagers, including 124 girls and 37 boys. All participants were selected because their answers on a questionnaire showed that they suffered from some level of distress and/or social anxiety. For instance, the teens all reported that they had difficulty making friends or relating to the friends they had. During the ten-week study, the students were divided into six groups, with four of the groups assigned blogging responsibilities at least twice per week. Two of the blogging groups were told to focus their posts on social problems, and one of those would be open to comments from visitors. The other two blogging groups could write about whatever they wanted, with one of them also open to comments. The remaining two groups collectively formed the control group, meaning no assignment was given to them. Those teens were told that they could write in a private diary about their social problems or opt not to write at all; the choice was up to them.

By the conclusion of the study, it was clear that blogging could help teens improve their self-esteem and enhance friendships. The researchers discovered that for the teens who were most troubled, writing about their struggles online was a more effective way to improve their self-esteem and their relationships than keeping a private journal. This, the researchers theorize, could be because the interactivity of a blog is beneficial for teens in overcoming social anxiety. Study coauthor Azy Barak writes: "Although cyber-bullying and online abuse are extensive and broad, we noted that almost all responses to our participants' blog messages were supportive and positive in nature. We weren't surprised, as we frequently see positive social expressions online in terms of generosity, support and advice."[79]

> " When young people are troubled, including suffering from problems at home, at school, in relationships, or just life in general, mental health professionals often encourage them to keep a journal. "

A Challenge Well Worth Pursuing

Studies have consistently shown that high stress is common among teens today. Contrary to what is often believed, however, it is not inevitable.

> **There are many ways for young people to reduce stress levels and keep them under control.**

There are many ways for young people to reduce stress levels and keep them under control, including practicing yoga, participating in exercise programs, getting more sleep, and/or writing in a journal or blog. These and other stress management strategies are important for teens to know about—but according to the APA's *Stress in America* survey, many are not aware of it. More than 42 percent of teens said they were not doing anything to cope with their stress and/or did not know how. As awareness continues to grow about high stress levels among young people, more teens will undoubtedly be motivated to learn about and adopt stress management techniques that improve their quality of life.

How Can Teens Cope with Stress?

Regardless of the high levels of stress that teens report and the symptoms of stress they report experiencing, they often do not know what to do to manage their stress.

—American Psychological Association, *Stress in America: Are Teens Adopting Adults' Stress Habits?*, February 11, 2014.
www.apa.org.

The APA is America's largest scientific and professional organization representing the field of psychology.

....

The most effective way to manage stress is to manage lifestyle and complement it with specific stress-busting strategies.

—Rick Harrington, *Stress, Health and Well-Being: Thriving in the 21st Century*. Belmont, CA: Wadsworth, 2013, p. 17.

Harrington is a psychologist, researcher, and university professor from Houston, Texas.

....

* Editor's Note: While the definition of a primary source can be narrowly or broadly defined, for the purposes of Compact Research, a primary source consists of: 1) results of original research presented by an organization or researcher; 2) eyewitness accounts of events, personal experience, or work experience; 3) first-person editorials offering pundits' opinions; 4) government officials presenting political plans and/or policies; 5) representatives of organizations presenting testimony or policy.

> **❝Teens that develop a 'relaxation response' and other stress management skills feel less helpless and have more choices when responding to stress.❞**

—American Academy of Child & Adolescent Psychiatry, "Helping Teenagers Deal with Stress," February 2013. www.aacap.org.

Representing nearly nine thousand child and adolescent psychiatrists, the American Academy of Child & Adolescent Psychiatry seeks to promote the health and well-being of children, adolescents, and families.

> **❝Awareness is a big step in becoming free of the stress created by believing our fears and other negative thoughts.❞**

—Gina Lake, *From Stress to Stillness: Tools for Inner Peace*. Sedona, AZ: Endless Satsang Foundation, 2013, p. viii.

Lake holds a master's degree in counseling psychology and has written a number of books about stress, wellness, and happiness.

> **❝No matter what stresses you out, there are many things you can try to help you deal.❞**

—Office on Women's Health, "Feeling Stressed," April 9, 2014. http://girlshealth.gov.

The Office on Women's Health works to improve the health and well-being of women and girls in the United States.

> **❝There's no quick-fix approach to minimizing stress, but stress recovery is possible. It begins with awareness.❞**

—Lori Lite, *Stress Free Kids*. Avon, MA: Adams Media, 2014, p. 21.

Lite is a certified children's meditation facilitator, author, and founder of the Marietta, Georgia–based group Stress Free Kids.

66 For many people exercise is an extremely effective stress buster. 99

—Christian Nordqvist, "What Is Stress? How to Deal with Stress," Medical News Today, July 30, 2014. www.medicalnewstoday.com.

Nordqvist is cofounder and editor of Medical News Today.

....

66 Fortunately, research is showing that lifestyle changes and stress-reduction techniques can help people manage stress. 99

—University of Maryland Medical Center, "Stress," June 26, 2013. http://umm.edu.

Located in downtown Baltimore, the University of Maryland Medical Center is one of the oldest academic medical centers in the United States.

....

66 In order to reduce the likelihood that stress even arises, it is imperative to create stress management skills. These skills increase our overall relaxation capacity. 99

—Henri Roca, interviewed by two high school students, "Teen Stress—an Interview," Dr. Henri Roca, February 13, 2013. http://drhenriroca.com.

Roca is a family medicine physician from Greenwich, Connecticut.

....

How Can Teens Cope with Stress?

- According to the APA's 2014 *Stress in America* study, **39 percent** of teens reported skipping exercise or physical activity when they felt stressed.

- **Four out of five teens** with mental health disorders do not seek treatment, due to the social stigma associated with having such a disorder, according to the mental health advocacy group Minding Your Mind.

- According to a 2014 article in *Psychology Today*, humor helps strengthen the immune system, reduce pain, and lower stress levels, as well as reduce feelings of anger, depression, and anxiety.

- The Center for Mental Health Services states that early intervention in mental health disorders greatly reduces the chance that an adolescent will engage in risky behavior and also reduces the likelihood that symptoms will return later in life.

- A 2012 Harris Interactive survey found that teens are more likely than other generations to use sedentary behaviors such as eating, spending time online, and playing video games to manage stress, and the majority of teens listen to music to cope.

- According to the Centers for Disease Control and Prevention, at least **90 percent** of people who commit suicide have a treatable mental illness.

Many Ways of Coping

Before stress becomes overwhelming, teens can benefit from learning how to get it under control and manage it. Shown here are stress management skills recommended by the Johns Hopkins Bloomberg School of Public Health.

- Talk about problems with others.

- Take deep breaths, accompanied by thinking or saying aloud, "I can handle this."

- Perform progressive muscle relaxation, which involves repeatedly tensing and relaxing large muscles of the body.

- Set small goals and break tasks into smaller, manageable chunks.

- Exercise and eat regular meals.

- Get proper sleep.

- Break the habit of relying on caffeine or energy drinks to get through the day.

- Visualize and practice feared situations.

- Focus on what you can control (your reactions, your actions) and let go of what you cannot (other people's opinions and expectations).

- Work through worst-case scenarios until they seem amusing or absurd.

- Lower unrealistic expectations.

- Schedule breaks and enjoyable activities.

- Accept yourself as you are; identify your unique strengths and build on them.

- Give up on the idea of perfection, both in yourself and in others.

Source: Johns Hopkins Bloomberg School of Public Health, "Teen Stress," *The Teen Years Explained.* www.jhsph.edu.

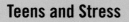

Calming Words

During a 2013 online survey, teens were asked about what inspires them and makes them feel better when they feel stressed-out. Their responses are shown here.

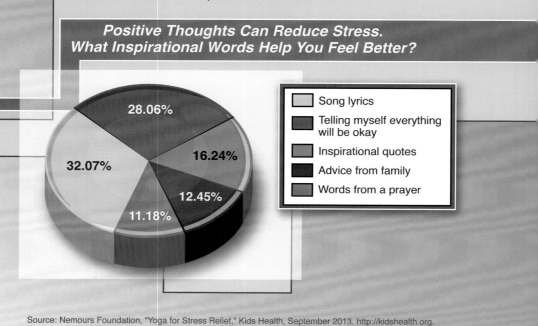

Positive Thoughts Can Reduce Stress. What Inspirational Words Help You Feel Better?

28.06%
16.24%
32.07%
12.45%
11.18%

- Song lyrics
- Telling myself everything will be okay
- Inspirational quotes
- Advice from family
- Words from a prayer

Source: Nemours Foundation, "Yoga for Stress Relief," Kids Health, September 2013. http://kidshealth.org.

- Between **70 and 90 percent** of people who use therapy and medication as a way to cope with their mental health disorder experience a reduction in symptoms, according to the mental health advocacy group Minding Your Mind.

- A 2012 study done by researchers from Harvard Medical School and Brigham and Women's Hospital found that teens who took yoga classes scored better on various psychosocial tests than teens who did not take yoga classes, which suggests that yoga may improve adolescent mental health.

- In a 2014 *Los Angeles Times* article, APA chief executive Norman Anderson stated that parents should model healthy stress management behavior such as regular exercise and adequate sleep to help their stressed teen.

- The website WebMD reports that a healthy diet can help reduce stress by increasing levels of serotonin, lowering levels of cortisol and adrenaline, lowering blood pressure, and boosting the immune system.

- A 2013 study reported in the journal *Health Psychology* found that mindfulness training—including meditation, mindful breathing, observation skills, and cultivation of positive attitudes like compassion—helped decrease levels of the stress hormone cortisol.

- Research suggests that meditation may alter the brain's neural pathways and make people more resilient to stress, according to psychologist Robbie Maller Hartman, a Chicago health and wellness coach.

Key People and Advocacy Groups

American Academy of Child & Adolescent Psychiatry: Composed of nearly nine thousand psychiatrists and other physicians, the academy's members research, evaluate, diagnose, and treat mental health disorders, including those that are stress related.

American Institute of Stress: An organization that serves as a clearinghouse of stress-related information, covering topics such as stress reduction, stress in the workplace, and effects of stress.

American Psychological Association: A scientific and professional organization that represents the field of psychology in the United States.

Walter Bradford Cannon: An American physiologist who was the first to recognize that stressors could be emotional as well as physical; it was also Cannon who discovered that animals, including humans, have an instinctive fight-or-flight mechanism.

Sheldon Cohen: A Carnegie Mellon University professor of psychology who is widely recognized for his research on the relationship between stress and the immune system, and how high stress can lead to illness.

Richard Earle: A scientist and stress expert who cofounded the Canadian Institute of Stress along with renowned stress researcher Hans Selye.

Thomas Holmes and Richard Rahe: American psychiatrists who studied thousands of patient medical records and concluded that stress contributes to illness; in 1967 they published a standardized measure of the impact of numerous stressors called the Social Readjustment Rating Scale.

Janice Kiecolt-Glaser and Ronald Glaser: Kiecolt-Glaser, a psychologist at the Ohio State University College of Medicine, and Glaser, an immunologist at Ohio State University, are widely recognized for nearly thirty years of research examining the link between stress and weakened immune system function.

Richard S. Lazarus: A professor emeritus of psychology at the University of California–Berkeley who is known for his stress research and detailed monograph titled *Psychological Stress and the Coping Process.*

Mental Health America: The United States' oldest advocacy organization devoted to mental health.

National Institute of Mental Health: An agency of the US Department of Health and Human Services and the largest research organization in the world specializing in mental illness.

Florence Nightingale: A British social reformer and founder of modern nursing, Nightingale wrote about patients who suffered from stress (although it was not yet called that) in her 1860 book, *Notes on Nursing.*

Hans Selye: A world-renowned scientist and cofounder of the Canadian Institute of Stress, Selye devoted much of his career to studying stress and is often called the "father of stress research."

Chronology

1966
Richard S. Lazarus, a professor of psychology at the University of California–Berkeley and a noted stress researcher, publishes his influential monograph titled *Psychological Stress and the Coping Process*.

1860
British social reformer Florence Nightingale publishes a book called *Notes on Nursing: What It Is, and What It Is Not*, in which she observes that all patients suffer from distress, with its own set of symptoms, regardless of what disease they have.

Late 1950s
American cardiologists Meyer Friedman and Ray Rosenman create the Type A personality concept, which defines a high-stress person who is especially vulnerable to disease.

1936
In a short article published in the scientific journal *Nature*, Hungarian-born scientist Hans Selye describes his experiments with animals and explains the harmful effects of stress on their bodies.

1850

1950

1915
In his book *Bodily Changes in Pain, Hunger, Fear and Rage*, American physiologist Walter Bradford Cannon describes how animals have an instinct for sensing potential threats that he refers to as the fight-or-flight response.

1953
In his book *Stress and Disease*, American neurologist Harold G. Wolff proposes a holistic model of stress in which both psychological and physiological factors are involved.

1967
After studying thousands of patient medical records and concluding that stress contributes to illness, psychiatrists Thomas Holmes and Richard Rahe publish a standardized measure of the impact of numerous stressors called the Social Readjustment Rating Scale.

1952
The first edition of the American Psychiatric Association's *Diagnostic and Statistical Manual of Mental Disorders* is published, ushering in the formal classification of modern mental illnesses. Included is the diagnosis "gross stress reaction," which is later renamed "post-traumatic stress disorder."

1968
The diagnosis "gross stress reaction" is dropped from the second edition of the DSM.

1980
Post-traumatic stress disorder is named as an official psychiatric illness in the third edition of the DSM.

2000
Researchers from the University of California–Los Angeles identify a biological and behavioral pattern that explains why females tend to respond to stress differently than males.

2013
The American Psychiatric Association releases the fifth version of the *Diagnostic and Statistical Manual of Mental Disorders*, which includes for the first time a chapter titled "Trauma- and Stressor-Related Disorders."

1990
At the annual meeting of the Society of Behavioral Medicine in Chicago, Illinois, researchers present a study showing that a stress reduction technique known as mindfulness meditation can help reduce symptoms of anxiety and panic in patients who suffer from anxiety disorders.

2010
The APA releases its third *Stress in America* survey, in which the majority of teens reported being strongly affected by their parents' stress.

1980   1990   2000   2010

1984
Psychologist Janice Kiecolt-Glaser and immunologist Ronald Glaser publish a paper titled "Psychosocial Modifiers of Immunocompetence in Medical Students," which describes their study showing the link between stress and weakened immune system function.

2009
A National Institute of Mental Health study reveals how individual cells adapt to cope with sudden or extreme stress and how repeated exposure to stress may be related to a number of physical and mental illnesses.

2004
The US Food and Drug Administration issues its most serious "black box" warning for all antidepressant drugs, due to the potential risk of increased suicidal thoughts and behaviors among children and adolescents.

2014
The APA releases a study titled *Stress in America: Are Teens Adopting Adults' Stress Habits?*, which shows that teens have higher stress levels than was previously known—in some cases even higher than adults' stress levels.

Related Organizations

American Academy of Child & Adolescent Psychiatry (AACAP)
3615 Wisconsin Ave. NW
Washington, DC 20016-3007
phone: (202) 966-7300 • fax: (202) 966-2891
website: www.aacap.org

Composed of more than eight thousand psychiatrists and other physicians, the AACAP's members actively research, evaluate, diagnose, and treat psychiatric disorders. Its website contains a section titled "Youth Resources" that includes a wealth of information for young people on coping with stress and finding help for themselves or their friends.

American Institute of Stress
9112 Camp Bowie West Blvd. #228
Fort Worth, TX 76116
phone: (682) 239-6823 • fax: (817) 394-0593
e-mail: info@stress.org • website: www.stress.org

The American Institute of Stress serves as a clearinghouse of stress-related information, including topics such as stress reduction, stress in the workplace, and effects of stress. Numerous stress-related materials are available on its website, which also contains links to the *Daily Life* blog and an online discussion forum.

American Psychological Association (APA)
750 First St. NE
Washington, DC 20002-4242
phone: (202) 336-5500; toll-free: (800) 374-2721
website: www.apa.org

The APA is a scientific and professional organization that represents the field of psychology in the United States. Its website links to newspaper articles, research data, and a number of online publications that focus on stress.

Centers for Disease Control and Prevention (CDC)

1600 Clifton Rd.
Atlanta, GA 30333
phone: (800) 232-4636
e-mail: cdcinfo@cdc.gov • website: www.cdc.gov

The CDC is a federal agency charged with protecting the health of Americans. Its website contains a section titled "Coping with Stress," which includes basic information, tips to help teens cope with stress, and numerous links to publications and other related organizations.

Mayo Clinic

200 First St. SW
Rochester, MN 55905
phone: (507) 284-2511
website: www.mayoclinic.org

The Mayo Clinic is a world-renowned health care facility and the largest nonprofit medical group practice in the world. Its website includes a section titled "Stress Management," which contains resources such as a newsletter, articles, tips on relaxation techniques, a stress blog, and numerous links to other websites and organizations that help individuals cope with stress.

Mental Health America

2000 N. Beauregard St., 6th Floor
Alexandria, VA 22311
phone: (703) 684-7722; toll-free: (800) 969-6642
fax: (703) 684-5968
e-mail: www.mentalhealthamerica.net/contact-us
website: www.mentalhealthamerica.net

Formed in 1909, Mental Health America is the nation's oldest advocacy organization that addresses mental health. Its website contains numerous resources related to stress, including basic facts, tools for reducing stress, tips on how to get help, and a stress screener.

Minding Your Mind (MYM)

42 W. Lancaster Ave., 2nd Floor
Ardmore, PA 19003
phone: (610) 642-3879 • fax: (610) 896-5704
e-mail: trish@mindingyourmind.org
website: http://mindingyourmind.org

MYM provides mental health education to children, teens, and young adults as well as parents, teachers, and school administrators. The organization offers educational programs that cover numerous issues, including stress. Its website provides several resources, including news, events, and a section on mental health basics for students.

National Alliance on Mental Illness (NAMI)

3803 N. Fairfax Dr., Suite 100
Arlington, VA 22203
phone: (703) 524-7600 • fax: (703) 524-9094
website: www.nami.org

NAMI is a nonprofit advocacy group for everyone affected by mental illness in the United States. Its website includes the Child & Adolescent Action Center, which works to improve the lives of children, teens, and young adults affected by mental illness.

National Child Traumatic Stress Network (NCTSN)

NCCTS—Duke University
411 W. Chapel Hill St., Suite 200
Durham, NC 27701
phone: (919) 682-1552 • fax: (919) 613-9898
website: www.nctsn.org

The NCTSN works to improve access to care, treatment, and services for children and teens exposed to traumatic events. Its website contains a multitude of resources, including information on the various types of traumatic stress, an e-bulletin, news, upcoming events, research, articles about children and traumatic stress, and numerous links for more information.

National Institute of Mental Health (NIMH)

6001 Executive Blvd., Room 6200, MSC 9663
Bethesda, MD 20892-9663
phone: (866) 615-6464 • fax: (301) 443-4279
website: www.nimh.nih.gov

An agency of the US Department of Health and Human Services, the NIMH is the largest research organization in the world specializing in mental illness. The website's "Child and Adolescent Mental Health" section contains news, studies, several publications for children and teens, information on types of treatment, a videocast, and several links for more information.

Office of Adolescent Health (OAH)

1101 Wootton Pkwy., Suite 700
Rockville, MD 20852
e-mail: oah.gov@hhs.gov
website: www.hhs.gov/ash/oah/adolescent-health-topics/mental-health

Part of the US Department of Health and Human Services, the OAH works to improve the health and well-being of teens. The OAH website contains numerous resources and publications, a section on adolescent mental health, a news feed, and links to outside organizations that can help teens deal with stress and other mental health issues.

We Are Talking!

Palo Alto Medical Foundation
795 El Camino Real
Palo Alto, CA 94301
phone: (650) 321-4121
website: www.pamf.org/teen

We Are Talking! consists of Palo Alto Medical Foundation physicians, social workers, educators, and researchers who are concerned with addressing the health care needs of teens. Its website provides information on teen health; tobacco, drug, and alcohol use; sexual health; anxiety and depression; and tips on coping with stress.

For Further Research

Books

Anthony R. Ciminero, *iCope: Building Resilience Through Stress Management*. Seattle, WA: CreateSpace, 2014.

Sean Covey, *The 7 Habits of Highly Effective Teens*. New York: Touchstone, 2014.

Al Desetta, ed., *Pressure: True Stories by Teens About Stress*. Minneapolis, MN: Free Spirit, 2012.

Robert Gallagher, *Stress Management: An Easy to Understand Book Full of Tips and Tricks to Fight Against Everyday Stress*. Seattle, WA: CreateSpace, 2013.

Gina Lake, *From Stress to Stillness: Tools for Inner Peace*. Sedona, AZ: Endless Satsang Foundation, 2013.

Laura Maciuika, *Conscious Calm: Keys to Freedom from Stress and Worry*. Oakland, CA: Tap Into Freedom, 2013.

Jason Porterfield, *Teen Stress and Anxiety*. New York: Rosen, 2014.

Christina Singh, *CHILLAX: Meditation for Teens*. Self-published, 2013. Kindle edition.

Amit Sood, *The Mayo Clinic Guide to Stress-Free Living*. Cambridge, MA: Da Capo, 2013.

Sarfraz Zaidi, *Stress Management for Teenagers, Parents and Teachers*. Camarillo, CA: iComet, 2013.

Periodicals

David Bornstein, "Protecting Children from Toxic Stress," *New York Times*, October 30, 2013.

Po Bronson and Ashley Merryman, "Why Can Some Kids Handle Pressure While Others Fall Apart?," *New York Times Magazine*, February 6, 2013.

Sharon Jayson, "Teens Feeling Stressed, and Many Not Managing It Well," *USA Today*, February 11, 2014.

Sharon Jayson, "Who's Feeling Stressed? Young Adults, New Survey Shows," *USA Today*, February 7, 2013.

Deborah Kotz, "Six Biggest Sources of Digital Stress in Teens," *Boston Globe*, July 25, 2014.

Laura McMullen, "Teen Stress: How Parents Can Help," *U.S. News & World Report*, February 17, 2014.

Donna Olmstead, "Activities Can Help Protect Stressed Teens," *Albuquerque Journal*, May 18, 2014.

Kimberly Palmer, "Survey: Teens Are Stressed over Money," *U.S. News & World Report*, March 28, 2014.

Alice Park, "America's Teens Outscore Adults on Stress," *Time*, February 11, 2014.

Andrew M. Seaman, "Stress Hormone Tied to Crash Risk Among Teens: Study," *Chicago Tribune*, April 8, 2014.

Jennifer Senior, "The Collateral Damage of a Teenager," *New York*, January 20, 2014.

Kelsey Thalhofer, "Workshop Helps Teens Face Stress Drug-Free," *Eugene (OR) Register Guard*, April 16, 2014.

Alexandra Thurmond, "Under Pressure: Teens Speak Out About Stress," *Teen Vogue*, March 2014.

Joanna Weiss, "Redefining Teenage Success," *Boston Globe*, April 25, 2014.

Internet Sources

American Academy of Child & Adolescent Psychiatry, "Helping Teenagers with Stress," February 2013. www.aacap.org/AACAP/Families_and_Youth/Facts_for_Families/Facts_for_Families_Pages/Helping_Teenagers_With_Stress_66.aspx.

Cincinnati Children's, "Coping with Teen Stressors." www.cincinnatichildrens.org/service/s/surviving-teens/coping.

Paula Davis-Laack, "Tapped Out Teens: 4 Stress Relief Strategies That Work," *Pressure Proof* (blog), *Psychology Today*, February 11, 2014.

www.psychologytoday.com/blog/pressure-proof/201402/tapped-out
-teens-4-stress-relief-strategies-work.

Rob Dunn, "What Are You So Scared Of? Saber-Toothed Cats, Snakes, and Carnivorous Kangaroos," *Slate*, October 15, 2012. www.slate .com/articles/health_and_science/human_evolution/2012/10/evo lution_of_anxiety_humans_were_prey_for_predators_such_as_hy enas_snakes.html.

Lucie Hemmen, "Stressed Out Teen Girls: Cutting to Cope," *Teen Girls: A Crash Course* (blog), *Psychology Today*, November 28, 2012. www.psychologytoday.com/blog/teen-girls-crash-course/201211 /stressed-out-teen-girls-cutting-cope.

Huffington Post, "Teen Stress," July 24, 2014. www.huffingtonpost.com /tag/teen-stress.

Lifespan, "Helping Teens Cope with Stress," 2014. www.lifespan.org /articles-and-tips/parenting/helping-teens-cope-with-stress.html.

Massachusetts Medical Society Alliance, "Teen Stress: Tips on Managing Daily Stress," 2012. www.massmed.org/About/Affiliates-and -Subsidiaries/MMS-Alliance/Teen-Stress--Tips-on-Managing-Daily -Stress-%28pdf%29.

Mayo Clinic, "Stress Management: Know Your Triggers," July 23, 2013. www.mayoclinic.org/healthy-living/stress-management/in-depth /stress-management/art-20044151.

Palo Alto Medical Foundation, "Stories About Coping," 2014. www .pamf.org/teen/life/stress/coping.

Kristen Race, "6 Ways to Help Your Teens Cope with Social Media Stress," *The Blog*, *Huffington Post*, March 13, 2014. www.huffington post.com/kristen-race-phd/6-ways-to-help-your-teens-cope-with -social-media-stress_b_4931490.html.

Erlanger A. Turner, "5 Tips for Helping Teens Cope with Stress," *The Race to Good Health* (blog), *Psychology Today*, February 22, 2014. www.psychologytoday.com/blog/the-race-good-health/201402 /5-tips-helping-teens-cope-stress.

Source Notes

Overview

1. Blake Kernen, "A Strong Case for a Snow Day Off," *Huffington Post*, February 5, 2014. www.huffingtonpost.com.
2. Kernen, "A Strong Case for a Snow Day Off."
3. Kernen, "A Strong Case for a Snow Day Off."
4. Kernen, "A Strong Case for a Snow Day Off."
5. Kernen, "A Strong Case for a Snow Day Off."
6. Johns Hopkins Bloomberg School of Public Health, "Teen Stress," *The Teen Years Explained*. www.jhsph.edu.
7. Hopkins Bloomberg School of Public Health, "Teen Stress."
8. Melissa Conrad Stöppler, "Stress," MedicineNet, September 4, 2013. www.medicinenet.com.
9. Christian Nordqvist, "What Is Stress? How to Deal with Stress," Medical News Today, July 30, 2014. www.medicalnewstoday.com.
10. Nordqvist, "What Is Stress? How to Deal with Stress."
11. Thea Singer, "The Perfect Amount of Stress," *Psychology Today*, May 18, 2012. www.psychologytoday.com.
12. Nemours Foundation, "Stress," TeensHealth, May 2013. http://kidshealth.org.
13. Nemours Foundation, "Stress."
14. Quoted in Patti Neighmond, "School Stress Takes a Toll on Health, Teens and Parents Say," *Shots* (blog), NPR, December 2, 2013. www.npr.org.
15. Nemours Foundation, "Stress."
16. Anonymous, "House of Stress," in *Pressure: True Stories by Teens About Stress*, ed. Al Desetta. Minneapolis, MN: Free Spirit, 2012, p. 18.
17. Anonymous, "House of Stress," p. 23.
18. University of Maryland Medical Center, "Stress," June 26, 2013. http://umm.edu.
19. American Academy of Pediatrics, "Study Explores Why Gay, Lesbian Teens Binge Drink," EurekAlert, May 3, 2014. www.eurekalert.org.
20. Quoted in Singer, "The Perfect Amount of Stress."
21. American Psychological Association, "Are Teens Adopting Adults' Stress Habits?," news release, February 11, 2014. www.apa.org.
22. Commission on Human Rights of Florida, "Teenage Stress—Dangers of Drug Abuse," October 21, 2011. www.cchrflorida.org.
23. American Psychological Association, "Are Teens Adopting Adults' Stress Habits?"
24. Quoted in Lucie Hemmen, "Stressed Out Teen Girls: Cutting to Cope," *Teen Girls: A Crash Course* (blog), *Psychology Today*, November 28, 2012. www.psychologytoday.com.
25. National Sleep Foundation, "Teens and Sleep." http://sleepfoundation.org.
26. Nemours Foundation, "Stress."

What Is Stress?

27. Quoted in Virginia Hill Rice, ed., *Handbook of Stress, Coping, and Health*. Thousand Oaks, CA: Sage, 2012. www.sagepub.com.

28. Quoted in Alix Spiegel, "The Secret History Behind the Science of Stress," NPR, July 7, 2014. www.npr.org.

29. Rice, *Handbook of Stress, Coping, and Health*.

30. Paul J. Rosch, "What Is Stress?," American Institute of Stress. www.stress.org.

31. American Academy of Child & Adolescent Psychiatry, "Helping Teenagers Deal with Stress," February 2013. www.aacap.org.

32. Walter Bradford Cannon, *Bodily Changes in Pain, Hunger, Fear and Rage*. New York: Appleton, 1915, p. 185.

33. Cannon, *Bodily Changes in Pain, Hunger, Fear and Rage*, p. 202.

34. Rob Dunn, "What Are You So Scared Of? Saber-Toothed Cats, Snakes, and Carnivorous Kangaroos," *Slate*, October 15, 2012. www.slate.com.

35. Harvard Medical School, "Understanding the Stress Response," *Harvard Mental Health Letter*, March 2011. www.health.harvard.edu.

36. Harvard Medical School, "Understanding the Stress Response."

37. Harvard Medical School, "Understanding the Stress Response."

38. Claire McCarthy, "02 27 2014 Stressed Teens," Boston Children's Hospital, February 27, 2014. www.childrenshospital.org

39. McCarthy, "02 27 2014 Stressed Teens."

40. Quoted in NBC News, "Study: Teens Are Stressed Out," KSDK.com, February 11, 2014. www.ksdk.com.

What Causes Teens to Get Stressed?

41. Matt Lehrer, "Forced to Face College," in *Pressure: True Stories by Teens About Stress*, ed. Al Desetta. Minneapolis, MN: Free Spirit, p. 25.

42. Lehrer, "Forced to Face College," p. 25.

43. Lehrer, "Forced to Face College," p. 27.

44. Lehrer, "Forced to Face College," p. 28.

45. Quoted in Roni Cohen-Sandler, "Recognizing Effects of Stress on Girls," Family Education. http://life.familyeducation.com.

46. Quoted in Laura Bartusiak, Elani Kaufman, and Joe Hendrix, "Generation Stressed Out," *The Mash* (blog), April 14, 2014. http://themash.com.

47. Tommy M. Phillips, Brandy A. Randall, Donna J. Peterson, and Joe D. Wilmoth, "Personal Problems Among Rural Youth and Their Relation to Psychosocial Well-Being," *Journal of Extension*, June 2013. www.joe.org.

48. Phillips et al., "Personal Problems Among Rural Youth and Their Relation to Psychosocial Well-Being."

49. Nemours Foundation, "Dealing with Bullying," Teens Health, July 2013. http://kidshealth.org.

50. Nemours Foundation, "Dealing with Bullying."

51. Quoted in Laura Krantz, "Cyber-Bullying, Stress, Concerns Among Teens," *Framingham (MA) MetroWest Daily News*, December 6, 2013. www.metrowestdailynews.com.

52. Quoted in Vicki Abeles and Abigail Baird, "Sleep Deprivation and Teens: 'Walking Zombies,'" *Washington Post*, March 10, 2012. www.washingtonpost.com.

53. Quoted in Yasmin Anwar, "Teen Night Owls Likely to Perform Worse Academically, Emotionally," UC Berkeley News Center, November 10, 2013. http://newscenter.berkeley.edu.

What Health Problems Are Associated with Stress?

54. Quoted in American Academy of Pediatrics, "Teenagers and Headaches: When It's Cause for Concern," Healthy Children, May 29, 2014. www.healthychildren.org.

55. Quoted in Neighmond, "School Stress Takes a Toll on Health, Teens and Parents Say."

56. Saul McLeod, "Stress, Illness and the Immune System," Simply Psychology, 2010. www.simplypsychology.org.

57. Quoted in Katie Moisse, "Chronic Stress Feeds Common Cold, Study Finds," ABC News, April 2, 2012. http://abcnews.go.com.

58. Quoted in Shilo Rea, "Press Release: How Stress Influences Disease: Carnegie Mellon Study Reveals Inflammation as the Culprit," Carnegie Mellon News, April 2, 2012. www.cmu.edu.

59. American Psychological Association, "Stress Effects on the Body," 2014. www.apa.org.

60. American Psychological Association, "Stress Effects on the Body."

61. Nemours Foundation, "Irritable Bowel Syndrome," Teens Health, May 2013. http://kidshealth.org.

62. Nemours Foundation, "Irritable Bowel Syndrome."

63. Nicolle, "My Teenage Life with IBS: Advice Needed!," Irritable Bowel Syndrome Self Help and Support Group, May 15, 2012. www.ibsgroup.org.

64. Nicolle, "My Teenage Life with IBS."

65. Mayo Clinic, "Teen Depression," November 7, 2012. www.mayoclinic.org.

66. Quoted in Bill Hathaway, "Even in the Healthy, Stress Causes Brain to Shrink, Yale Study Shows," YaleNews, January 9, 2012. http://news.yale.edu.

67. Quoted in Chris Iliades, "Stress May Trigger Mental Illness and Depression in Teens," EverydayHealth.com, January 17, 2013. www.everydayhealth.com.

68. Quoted in Iliades, "Stress May Trigger Mental Illness and Depression in Teens."

How Can Teens Cope with Stress?

69. Henri Roca, interviewed by two high school students, "Teen Stress—an Interview," Dr. Henri Roca, February 13, 2013. http://drhenriroca.com.

70. Roca, interviewed by two high school students, "Teen Stress—an Interview."

71. Quoted in Alexandra Muller Arboleda, "Yoga: Serenity and Stress Relief for Teens," Raising Arizona Kids, January 2014. www.raisingarizonakids.com.

72. Quoted in Arboleda, "Yoga."

73. Quoted in Arboleda, "Yoga."

74. Anna Duberg, Lars Hagberg, Helena Sunvisson, and Margareta Möller, "Influencing Self-Rated Health Among Adolescent Girls with Dance Intervention," *JAMA Pediatrics*, 2013. http://archpedi.jamanetwork.com.

75. Adela Han, "How to Help Teens with Depression," *Chillin' Out* (blog), University of Texas, 2014. https://sites.utexas.edu.

76. Duberg et al., "Influencing Self-Rated Health Among Adolescent Girls with Dance Intervention."

77. Duberg et al., "Influencing Self-Rated Health Among Adolescent Girls with Dance Intervention."

78. Quoted in Rick Nauert, "Blogs May Help Teens Reduce Social Stress," Psych Central, January 5, 2012. http://psychcentral.com.

79. Quoted in Nauert, "Blogs May Help Teens Reduce Social Stress."

List of Illustrations

Index

Note: Boldface page numbers indicate illustrations.

About the Author

Peggy J. Parks holds a bachelor of science degree from Aquinas College in Grand Rapids, Michigan, where she graduated magna cum laude. An author who has written more than one hundred educational books for children and young adults, Parks lives in Muskegon, Michigan, a town that she says inspires her writing because of its location on the shores of Lake Michigan.